T0328472

True Change

Janice A. Klein

True Change

How Outsiders on the Inside Get
Things Done in Organizations

JOSSEY-BASS
A Wiley Imprint
www.josseybass.com

Published by Jossey-Bass
A Wiley Imprint
989 Market Street, San Francisco, CA 94103-1741   www.josseybass.com

Jossey-Bass books and products are available through most bookstores. To contact Jossey-Bass directly call our Customer Care Department within the U.S. at 800-956-7739, outside the U.S. at 317-572-3986 or fax 317-572-4002.

Jossey-Bass also publishes its books in a variety of electronic formats. Some content that appears in print may not be available in electronic books.

Library of Congress Cataloging-in-Publication Data
Klein, Janice, 1950-
  True change : how outsiders on the inside get things done in organizations / Janice Klein.—1st ed.
      p. cm.
  Includes bibliographical references and index.
  HB ISBN 0-7879-7473-0 (alk. paper)
  PB ISBN 978-1-119-11657-8

1. Organizational change. 2. Organizational effectiveness. 3. Corporate culture. 4. Employee motivation. I. Title.
  HD58.8.K568 2004
  658.4'06—dc22
                                        2004010943

FIRST EDITION
HB Printing   10 9 8 7 6 5 4 3 2 1
PB Printing   10 9 8 7 6 5 4 3 2 1

Contents

To all my students and colleagues who contributed to the research projects that are the backbone of this book

Preface

This book is the result of thirty years of experience and research. Throughout my career, I have attempted to facilitate the introduction of new ideas to improve organizations. The journey has not been easy; there have definitely been trials and tribulations along the way. But in all cases, they were opportunities to reflect, learn, and improve both practice and teaching. I began as an engineer, moved into supervisory and managerial roles, and eventually turned to academia and consulting work. That experience informed my research, which in turn informed my understanding of past success—and failure—in trying to introduce new ideas and concepts.

As such, *True Change* represents far more than academic ramblings. The combined power of people (outsiders on the inside), approach (pulling change), and system (support infrastructure) is more than a repackaging of traditional theories of change management. No one could write a book about change management without including many old nuggets of truth, of course, and these are noted throughout the chapters. But there is also something different about *True Change:* it is a process of systemic change that is framed in operational terms. It is a complex process that took over five years to formulate and document. I am grateful to one referee who recognized this and helped me to articulate that my book is about building a change capability, not just managing change.

Many of the concepts outlined in this book emerged while trying to make sense of the stories reported throughout the interviews that constituted much of my research. Others surfaced as students, alumni, and managers tried these ideas out in practice. These are ideas that have been tested and refined in the field. The mutuality of responsibility between outsiders on the inside and the organizations they attempt to change is a case in point. I have been an outsider on the inside, managed other outsiders on the inside, coached both them and their organizations as a consultant and teacher, and heard—and reflected on—their stories throughout the research.

The ability to wear two hats—one as a practitioner and the other as a teacher or researcher—is something I have tried to retain and apply throughout my work on this book. The final chapter on maintaining a balance between the outsider and insider hats is as much a reflection of my experience as it is the research. My own odyssey highlighted the need to ground *True Change* in the theories of academia but write it for practitioners—the doers who make change "true."

I have been fortunate to lead three outstanding teams of researchers exploring different but related aspects of creating true change. One explored the use of new perspectives in revitalizing manufacturing enterprises, another investigated global and virtual collaboration, and the third examined the introduction of a new paradigm of systems engineering. At first, these projects were distinct, but on reflection, I realized that the research subjects were all outsiders on the inside attempting to pull new ideas into their organizations. These projects were all conducted under the auspices of the Leaders for Manufacturing (LFM) and System Design and Management (SDM) Partnership, a partnership between MIT's School of Engineering, Sloan School of Management, and numerous international manufacturing and engineering enterprises (the appendix provides further background on the partnership and the three research projects) that in itself is an example of true change. Many of the examples throughout the book are evidence of the impact that LFM/SDM has had on numerous organizations in varied settings around the world.

True Change was written for executives, managers, and individuals in line organizations who are trying to introduce new ideas or alternative ways of doing things and want to institutionalize those concepts. The research was conducted predominantly in manufacturing and engineering environments, and the majority of the illustrations come from those industries as a result. But the ideas have applicability in just about any walk of life or line of business. Hence, the frameworks are relevant for organizational effectiveness and human resource professionals, as well as educators concerned with developing organizational leaders and change agents. Finally, consultants should take heed: it may appear that I attack the role that consultants play in introducing and disseminating new ideas. But I too function as a consultant and believe we play a valuable role. It is just that we ultimately cannot make things happen within our client organizations. We need outsiders on the inside to do that.

Acknowledgments

This book is a product of the contributions of many outsiders on the inside who graciously shared their stories, participated in the research process, and critiqued the analysis. Many were graduate students who both shared their diverse experiences and became research assistants for one of the three projects. Others were managers and alumni who became our field laboratory subjects. The number of contributors is so extensive that it would take many pages to identify them by name. I have chosen to dedicate this book to all of you in hopes that the dedication will be a greater honor than seeing your name in a long list of contributors. The dedication is my small way of saying thank you, since without you and the wisdom you shared, this book would never have become a reality.

There are, however, two individuals who deserve special recognition. The first is Bill Hanson, LFM/SDM industry codirector. He saw the value of my ideas, supported the research, pushed me to be relevant, and sacrificed more than a few Saturday morning golf games to read through volumes of early case studies and draft reports. Without his support and cheerleading over the past ten years, this book would never have seen the light of day. I also owe a debt of eternal gratitude to Barbara Feinberg. She has been an artful coach in helping me craft the story you are about to read and in prodding me to be more articulate and less cryptic in my writing, a never-ending, torturous process. It has been a pleasure and a blessing to work with her for close to twenty years.

Two additional outsiders on the inside deserve honorable mention. Roger Saillant and David Marsing somehow found time in their busy executive schedules to read through hundreds of pages of rambling cases and helped me formulate the ideas underlying the systemic nature of the pull change process and need for an organizational infrastructure to support outsiders on the inside. Those early discussions provided a foundation for further research and analysis.

I am grateful for the support of MIT and the LFM/SDM Partnership for making this book possible. All members of the partnership—industrial partners, students, faculty, and staff—have demonstrated the value of true collaboration between industry and academia and provided a safe haven for this nontraditional researcher. Special thanks go to the People Systems Network and all of the organizations that provided access for the research. This includes, but is not limited to, Boeing, Intel, Hewlett-Packard, Motorola, Alcoa, United Technologies, General Motors, Ford, Chrysler, Polaroid, Kodak, Digital, Visteon, ArvinMeritor, and NASA. Susan Williams and Jossey-Bass made the final stages of the writing journey much less painful than I could have ever imagined. I was pleased at how readily they supported my nonconventional approach to an old subject matter and didn't react with, "Oh, no, not another book on change management!"

Finally, this book is the product of another partnership—a very personal one. I have been blessed with a spouse who has listened to, contributed to, and tolerated endless discussions (sometimes heated debates) focused on the concepts that you are about to read. Dan, I don't know where your patience comes from, but I cherish your attempts to keep me grounded in the real world.

August 2004   Janice A. Klein

True Change

Chapter One

What Is True Change?

A full-page advertisement for a large international consulting firm pictured a line of empty airport pushcarts ready for luggage to be piled in by a passenger and wheeled along to a final destination. Each cart proudly displayed a placard reading, "I am your idea. Push me." The implication of this metaphor is that ideas just need to be bundled up like one's belongings and pushed along to be implemented. To me, this epitomized the problem with most change initiatives. Sure, there are plenty of success stories of how new ideas are deftly packaged and sold to hundreds of companies around the globe. These success stories are often accompanied by glowing accounts of how new concepts helped companies save billions of dollars. Unfortunately, a deeper look typically reveals that those new ideas lasted only as long as someone did the pushing. As soon as the champion for those new ideas moved on, the change initiative dissipated. This may be short-term change, but it isn't true change. True change occurs when ideas or concepts become embedded in the underlying assumptions about how work is done. True change means the new ideas become institutionalized and are no longer dependent on a change agent or champion to support them.

Many see the impetus for true change as a response to some external force. For example, something in the macro competitive or political environment forces the change to happen—the Internet bubble burst and caused the economy to take a nosedive, or global competition opened the door for a new look at supply chain management. Companies had to change to survive or face death by an unwelcome takeover or bankruptcy. Others might point to disruptive technologies as the driver of change, such as wireless communications that created opportunities for some organization but disaster for others.[1] But whether a firm grabs these forces and uses them to its advantage is something that happens internally. True change requires more than a set of well-crafted strategies and tactics pushed along by a charismatic leader. It is not just wheeling in a new set of ideas and then having another pushcart of other ideas waiting in line to deal with the next catastrophic event.

True change requires an adaptive change capability within a firm that neither springs up overnight nor depends on only a handful of "change agents" who push their ideas onto the organization. The people who create true change are inside the firm, not outside or solely at the top. They are employees at all levels, working in concert throughout the organization, who see opportunities for applying new ideas to solve problems at their workplace. In sum, true change is not just a random occurrence, with "forces" happening to be aligned so that the seeds for change turn into seedlings that mature into trees with roots that don't get ripped out with the next wind that comes along, be it (yet another) reorganization or (yet another) "program of the month." This book is about turning the successful implementation of new ideas into predictable events with predictable results. It is about matching new ideas or innovations to problems that need urgent attention. That sounds obvious, but doing it is another story.

True change joins three very basic concepts, each essential for successful implementation of new ideas but often missed because they are so basic. The first notion is that change occurs only from within. Outsiders, such as external consultants, can only recommend alternative approaches, not operationalize them. Second, ideas that are pushed on others are typically resisted. There needs to be a pull for new ideas to take hold, such as an unsolved challenge that current wisdom cannot overcome. Taking these points in combination results in the following: change occurs when insiders identify a specific challenge they are facing as an opportunity to pull in outside perspectives. I call people who are able to do this "outsiders on the inside," and they exist in every organization.[2] But local change typically has to fight significant organizational inertia and seldom survives continual attacks from the organization at large. So the third principle is that there needs to be a critical mass of outsiders on the inside to affect systemic change; one person alone cannot do it. Organizations must consciously create an environment that develops and nurtures outsiders on the inside who are aligned at all organizational levels.

Taken individually, these points may sound like old news, but their combined power emerged from analyzing the results of three interrelated research projects: (1) a study exploring the use of new manufacturing competencies in twelve major corporations, (2) an examination of virtual collaboration and the development of high-performance globally dispersed teams, and (3) an inquiry into the ability for full-time employees to learn new concepts through distance education while being totally emerged within their organizations' culture.[3] In each project, a key issue we uncovered was the strong desire of people within organizations to improve the work being done and their recognition of gaps between current organizational assumptions and what they saw as root causes for the challenges that faced their organizations. I realized that these inside people were able to see past their organizations' cultural assumptions and observe their challenges as an outsider might do. In other words, they held outsider perspectives, but they were not true outsiders: they were outsiders on the inside of their organizations. I also saw they needed a new framework to help them leverage that ability, which led to the notion that true change is pulled in by challenges, as opposed to being pushed by champions.

We saw that true change can occur at any level of the organization and is not dependent on a senior-level change initiative champion. Granted, such a person helps in some organizational cultures, but that support only greases the skids; it's not what makes the change happen. It is also not enough for the general demand for change to be seen in the abstract, and it is not enough to be provided with suggestions by outsiders like consultants or academics, even if these are mandated from above. Nor is a sense of urgency sufficient for true change to take hold. Just knowing that there is a need for change is insufficient. People need to see a tangible need and application for alternative ways of doing things. Only outsiders on the inside can see what needs to be done and how it can be accomplished in terms of the specific challenge. In other words, pushing change is general purpose, while pulling it is specific to a situation.

Finding opportunities that allow true change to be pulled in at the workplace is a role that can be played only by insiders within an organization who can step back and wear two hats: an insider's and an outsider's. Throughout the remainder of this book, I refer to these employees as *outsider-insiders* because they are both an insider and an outsider at the same time. As an insider, they understand the day-to-day ins and outs of the organization. They care deeply about their organization and want to improve it. Yet while they are comfortable working within the existing culture, they are also able to step back and see where internal assumptions about how work is done are getting in the way of optimal performance. They are the people who grab new ideas and make them work to help solve problems they face.

The processes that lead to true change are not an abstract set of steps: they are part of a strategy for building a change capability into the organization through developing and nurturing outsider-insiders and then deploying and using them to introduce new ways of working.[4] In doing so, there is a mutuality of responsibility shared by outsider-insiders and their organizations, and this is a theme that weaves throughout the book. As such, we look at the processes for creating true change from two perspectives: (1) that of managers who want to develop and better use outsider-insiders to help transform their organizations to better meet strategic objectives and (2) that of current or future outsider-insiders who are attempting to bring outsider ideas into their organization to make them more competitive. It takes both perspectives working in concert to create true change.

Although outsider-insiders are the ones who apply their outsider perspectives to address daily challenges, many of them need help in getting to the right place at the right time to find opportunities to pull in new ideas aligned with strategic objectives. They also need support in maintaining and honing their abilities. This means that organizations that want true change must create infrastructures to support the development and maintenance of outsider-insider capabilities, a subject we turn to in the second half of the book. But first we must understand the framework for how outsider-insiders go about making things happen in their organizations. For many, it is intuitively obvious, but managers, consultants, and academics continually ignore the obvious as they package ideas and pile them into their pushcarts.

What True Change Is Not

It's easy to change; people do it all the time. Volumes have been written about change management and how to overcome resistance to change, build a vision of what's possible, and get buy-in for the desired change.[5] Many of these strategies work, but all too often, the changes are short-lived or just cosmetic. Employees go through the motions in response to a new initiative or a push from a change agent. Once the change agent leaves, the pressure is off, and it's back to the old ways of doing things or on to the next change. Granted, there has been change but not true change. Take a look at the following example.[6]

The CEO of Worldwide Manufacturing Industries returned from an executive seminar on the importance of human resources in the introduction of lean manufacturing and immediately sent his chief knowledge officer (CKO) on a benchmarking trip of companies considered to be best practice examples. At the end of his investigation, the CKO recommended that Worldwide select a pilot facility to introduce these new concepts and serve as a model for the rest of the corporation. The Chicago plant was chosen because it was about to introduce a new product line and would provide a ready opportunity to showcase the new lean concepts. The CEO discussed the possibility of turning the Chicago operation into a model facility with the plant's division general manager, who readily agreed.

Rumors of the "lean model" plan soon filtered down to the Chicago plant. The first official validation came four months later when the CKO visited the facility to conduct a "readiness survey" that asked the plant's staff to describe improvements made in the past and where they perceived further opportunities to lie. Shortly after, a new plant manager was assigned to Chicago because the division's upper management felt he was the type of leader needed to create the model facility. His arrival came as a surprise to the plant employees, many of whom were upset that the current plant manager, who had won the respect, admiration, and loyalty of many people, was being replaced. To people within the plant, the new plant manager was viewed with suspicion because he came from corporate headquarters. In addition, he had no background in the plant's manufacturing processes.

The new plant manager organized a brainstorming session with his staff where he asked each manager to submit a set of notes defining his or her views of the model facility. Two months later, the CKO came back to the plant to conduct the first in a series of formal training programs. The training was received with mixed reviews. One participant noted, "Some of this training is just hype. There's a point where you're overdoing it. The training was boring at first; at the end, it was like, 'Let's get pumped up about the new buzzword.'" Subsequently, all salaried employees within the plant sat through a two-hour introduction to lean manufacturing practices.

Following the initial training, the CKO assisted the plant staff in developing a lean implementation plan. Staff members also became participants in a Lean Steering Committee along with the plant manager and the CKO. Shortly after, the plant's hourly workforce officially heard about lean when the division's general manager held one of his regular quarterly meetings at the Chicago plant and mentioned that the facility had been chosen to become a model operation. Two months later, the plant's manufacturing manager presented a half-hour talk to the hourly workforce, formally introducing the lean model concept.

Not surprisingly, the plant personnel had mixed feelings about the entire lean concept and what it would mean to the facility. The plant manager noted about six months later: "One problem with all the changes in becoming a lean model is that it has tended to take the fun out of work. Managers and workers like to have a crisis to handle every thirty days or so. Supervisors won't change overnight. Some have to retire because we won't be able to change their attitudes. Some of the staff probably feels the same way." In fact, the manufacturing manager was overheard to say, "Lean is not anything any different than what we've been doing for the past four or five years basically. All we have now is the visibility and a few more resources than before. It's a little frustrating at times because we felt we were already doing a lot of things." A supervisor voiced similar sentiments: "I don't know what lean means. No one in the shop really talks about lean. It's the same old thing we've been doing with a few new directions here and there."

Sound familiar? This is a scenario played out in various ways in just about every large organization. The CEO picked up a new idea he thought would improve the corporation's overall competitiveness and followed a widely recognized path of establishing a learning pilot that could be a launchpad for transforming the entire organization.

In many respects, Worldwide is a textbook example of following best practices in organizational change: gaining senior management commitment; cascading the new idea down through the organization to get each level of the hierarchy on board; installing a new local leader with a vision; benchmarking other organizations; providing extensive training; setting up a steering committee that bridges key stakeholders; and so on. But unfortunately, the result was all too predictable. The folks who ultimately had to introduce the new idea at the workplace level managed to reframe what they were currently doing to fit the new buzzwords. Many would label their reaction as good old-fashioned resistance to change, but these folks could justify their response by saying: "Here comes the latest flavor of the month!" Corporate management sold the idea to them as an opportunity to be a showcase, but to them it meant having to change behaviors that, from their perspective, *didn't need to change*. And from the CEO's perspective, the challenge—the introduction of lean manufacturing practices—remained.

So what was missing? Most change consultants would quickly point out that the plant lacked ownership. In other words, the CEO saw a need for change, but the people within the plant did not. Although the CEO's team made every attempt to educate the plant personnel and involve them in the change process, lean came across as an idea being pushed on them from the outside (corporate) by the new plant manager from corporate who didn't understand what the plant did and also was the reason their beloved prior plant manager was ousted. The CEO's attempt to introduce a new concept into his organization is a classic case of *pushcart change*.

Large organizations typically push change in various ways. There is the subtle push of someone just sharing a perspective with a friend or colleague. In many respects, this is how the CEO learned about lean concepts and then shared the idea with the CKO. At the other end of the push continuum are corporate edicts that are usually more like a shove or dump than a gentle nudge: this is how the Chicago personnel felt about the lean concept. And even corporate education programs aimed at building an understanding for the need for change often end up being viewed as preaching the company gospel, a sentiment voiced by participants in the lean training program. Between these bookends are the internal and external consultants who are selling and marketing new ideas; the CKO played such a role in helping to introduce lean into the Chicago plant. In fact, as this book argues over and over, the actual implementation and diffusion of new ideas takes hold only when the receiver pulls in the new concept to address a local challenge. That is what was missing in the Chicago plant case.

Pulling Change

Pulling change rather than pushing it is analogous to pulling versus pushing inventory. The theory behind pull inventory is that a workstation should produce a widget only when a customer indicates that one is needed. This avoids wasted effort associated with excess inventory that adds cost, hides quality problems, and becomes obsolete. For pulling change, the theory is quite similar: ideas are put in place only when there is a challenge that the current knowledge and experience base cannot adequately address. If there is no challenge, either real or perceived, pushing change just leads to wasted efforts.

The receiver of a change, like the downstream workstation, must recognize the need for a different approach than is currently being used. For example, a manager might see the inefficiencies of organizing work so it flows haphazardly among three work groups. But if the groups are meeting their objectives and their customers are not complaining, an idea to improve productivity will probably fall on deaf ears because everyone appears to be happy with the status quo. In other words, this would be just pushing change on to a nonexistent problem. Pulling change, in contrast, starts when the end users, that is, the people who need to change their behavior or how the current operation functions, recognize a gap between their current knowledge base or approach and what is needed to achieve their objectives. As an internal consultant in charge of implementing common processes across a plant network noted, "At first glance, it looks like these practices are pushed down from the top. But it wouldn't work that way. There is too much resistance. So we follow the pull strategy. We wait to hear from the plant management requesting help. . . . Oh yes, it has to be a pull!"

In many respects, ideas are the brain's inventory. Ideas reap benefits only when they get put into use to solve a business challenge. That challenge might be a thorny problem that the organization cannot solve with its current warehouse of knowledge, or it might be an urgent need to improve operations to stay ahead of the competition. In other words, ideas are useful only when someone takes an idea and solves a challenge being faced. The challenge, in essence, is the pull for implementing the ideas.

The challenge, however, must be something that the people who have to implement the change personally identify with. Neither the CKO (as the CEO's messenger) nor the new plant manager truly understood the challenges facing the Chicago plant's workforce on a daily basis. As a result, they were unable to find workplace challenges where lean would help shop floor employees overcome those daily impediments. The fact that the CEO had a challenge that lean would help solve was too removed from their daily lives. What the CKO and the plant manager should have done was find or develop outsider-insiders within the Chicago plant who could find workplace challenges that would pull in the lean manufacturing practices. This is the work of someone on the inside (*not* a corporate consultant or a newcomer to the plant) who is positioned to see what specific change has to be pulled where (that is, where the need "really" is).

Pure insiders have no reason to question their own assumptions; they are comfortable. Even when they encounter problems, their reaction is that the problem is elsewhere or they just have to do a better job of doing what they have been doing. It's like putting bigger and bigger bandages on a wound when it doesn't stop bleeding. Insiders may see the problems and have ideas on how to correct them, but they don't necessarily see the root cause because they are looking through their organization's cultural lenses. They don't question the system; they are totally entrenched in their organization's routines and just accept the way things are.

Traditional socialization processes can easily keep people from being able to step back and be objective about why they do what they do. Insiders experience the world they live within based on their organization's cultural assumptions. Indeed, for an organization to hold together and function efficiently, its members must share a core set of assumptions. If they didn't, chaos would reign, with people constantly questioning one another and moving in millions of different directions. So shared assumptions are critical. But sometimes those assumptions get in the way. As one supervisor noted about a college intern, "As an outsider, he put his finger on a lot of the problems right away that I knew but didn't really recognize because I was an insider."

Being on the outside, or new to an organization, facilitates seeing potential gaps between an establishment's current assumptions and the root cause of a challenge facing the business; the view is not blocked by internal cultural blinders. But while outsiders, such as external consultants, can observe gaps, their impact is limited to suggesting alternative approaches. It ultimately takes an insider to translate the applicability of those outsider views and apply them to a specific challenge facing their workplace.

The people who facilitate the process of finding opportunities to pull in new ideas are outsider-insiders. As one veteran outsider-insider who had a successful track record of introducing multiple new ideas explained, "In order to survive, you have to wear two hats: you have to be accepted as in insider but you have to have an outsider's view to see the gaps. Success is dependent on wearing two hats. If you only have one, you can't make change. If you're only an insider, you're stuck in the ways of doing things; if you're only an outsider, no one will listen to you."

As this outsider-insider described, insiders typically do not believe or trust that outsiders truly understand what it is really like within the organization. Outsiders, to both a specific operation (such as the Chicago plant) and the organization at large, rarely appreciate the entire set of norms and beliefs that underlies a work unit's culture. Understanding why people within an organization act the way they do requires a much deeper insight. It takes living within a system to fully understand the complexities and subtleties of a culture. This is where outsider-insiders play a pivotal role in introducing new ideas or processes. By their very nature, they are able to see connections that pure insiders miss because they have a different way of seeing the world or explaining why things appear to happen as they do. They are able to see where existing paradigms are the root cause of their organization's inability to accept new ideas or processes. At the same time, they are able to leverage the existing culture by living within the organization, another theme that is in the creation of true change.

As we will see throughout this book, introducing alternative perspectives into an organization is about more than just having and then implementing an out-of-the-box idea. It's about observing and using new and different methods to solve existing challenges that represent critical business needs. Those new approaches need to be grounded in a set of assumptions that attack the root cause of persistent challenges—root causes that are masked or overlooked by the existing organizational assumptions. Very few concepts or ideas are truly revolutionary. Occasionally someone will come up with an innovative concept, but for the most part, most ideas already exist somewhere in the universe. It is just that the mental models that would receive them within the organization where the idea is being introduced are rare.

Many opportunities to pull in change are challenges that are apparent to people within the organization, but current approaches to remedy them have failed to yield results. These present the easiest opportunities for pulling in new ideas. These problems may be a stand-alone issue or linked to broader strategic initiatives, for example, Worldwide's goal of introducing lean manufacturing. In the latter case, outsider-insiders provide the conduit for cascading new concepts throughout the organization. But there are also the "invisible" challenges ticking along as time bombs. These are often environmental changes that are obvious to outsiders but have yet to become visible to those inside. In many respects, these are the thorniest ones for outsider-insiders. These people not only have to help others see alternative viewpoints but must also help others to see the challenges confronting the organization. For outsider-insiders, all of these challenges look the same, but getting others to accept outsider perspectives is quite different.

Attacking a large organization head-on is a death wish, of course. It is well known that it is best to start with small wins that can eventually mushroom into large-scale change.[7] But how does one identify and find situations that can produce those small wins that get the ball rolling? Worldwide's approach obviously did not work. The problem is that there are way too many ideas or changes being pushed on employees. When someone has or hears about an idea or innovation that seems powerful, he or she tends to try to convince others within the organizations that the idea should be implemented. As we saw with the CEO's attempt to introduce lean, ideas that are pushed on people occasionally get heard but typically are not owned. It is relatively easy to modify behavior in response to a program of the month or put up with a supervisor you know is a short-timer. But real change in behavior typically requires a new perspective and a reexamination of the assumptions we hold that lead us to behave as we do. Granted, new behaviors can emerge from forced repetition (a push) that becomes habit, but buy-in and understanding when and why those behaviors are appropriate is often lacking.

Although there is no shortage of resistant individuals and organizations, the downfall in introducing new ideas is often in the approach taken. Outsider-insiders have the potential to teach others to see a different perspective as well as help them adopt alternative approaches. But outsider-insiders must first learn when and how to introduce their ideas effectively. It often takes patience to find just the right opportunity to introduce "countercultural" perspectives. Unfortunately, many change advocates are overly anxious to get others to see their perspectives, and they get ostracized for being too pushy. Many see themselves as change agents, but in reality, they aren't the agents of change. Rather, it's the challenge they are trying to overcome that provides the impetus for introducing their outsider perspectives.

As we will see, outsider-insiders facilitate true change by being in the right place at the right time to observe an opportunity that will pull in alternative approaches and having the skills and a process to lead the pulling in of those ideas to solve the problem. Some might argue that a problem needs to be large enough to gain attention, but all that is really necessary is that the targeted challenge be important and of some urgency to a subset of individuals. Strategically targeted small wins can grow by serving as a lever for building credibility for the new approaches. Put another way, these wins grease the way and reduce some of the friction in the pull system. The grease monkeys are the outsider-insiders who identify and lubricate the system! Their perspectives are basically tools that help others solve key organizational challenges.[8]

Outsider-Insiders Across All Levels of the Hierarchy

It is important to continually remember that outsider-insiders exist at all levels of an organization's hierarchy. Senior-level executives who champion new concepts or strategies are themselves outsider-insiders. Their viewpoint is typically strategic, and their focus is on systemwide policies and procedures. As such, they can provide overall sponsorship and protection for new perspectives, but their position within organizations usually prevents them from dealing with micro-level behavioral changes—the myriad day-to-day activities that aggregate into strategic transformations. They need supporting outsider-insiders who constitute a network of people observing daily challenges that provide opportunities for new ideas to be pulled in and applied. In other words, senior executives are the ones who develop strategic objectives to empower outsider-insiders throughout their organizations, but they must leave the hands-on doing to others. These senior managers also play a pivotal role in nurturing a supportive culture for fellow outsider-insiders by being champions and teachers of alternative perspectives.

Senior executives have the luxury of picking, mentoring, and, to some extent, protecting outsider-insiders, but individuals helping to introduce new ideas from the middle and lower levels of the organizational hierarchy must somehow identify people who are sympathetic to their perspectives. Although counter to conventional thinking, there are many outsider-insiders in the often disparaged ranks of middle management. Their peers are typically viewed as the blockers of change, but lurking in the shadows are patient (and sometimes impatient) advocates of new and different ways of doing things. As one outsider-insider in a middle management role noted,

> We have what we call the "ring of openness" in the middle of the organization. We make informal connections, often over coffee. We run into each other and figure out that we are allies. . . . The "ring of openness" is comprised of the folks who drive for change; they are the creative belt and it's basically "managing your boss." Below the "ring of openness" is the rest of the organization that is basically mixed. Their reaction when we suggest a change is, "Top management will never approve that." We basically get enough support within the "ring of openness" and then go together to top management. We build support one-on-one with members of upper management before we go to them as a group. At that point, it is hard for them to say no.

In addition to personally being outsider-insiders, these key supporters of change help to pave the way for others within their organizations. Middle managers can match frontline outsider-insiders to problems that need outsider perspectives. And like their executives, they can coach and mentor working-level outsider-insiders in the ins and outs of navigating complex organizations and effectively introducing new concepts.

Then there are the frontline outsider-insiders. These are the folks who see daily challenges ripe for applying alternative assumptions to solve critical problems. Some are lucky enough to work in organizations that value and support outsider perspectives, but most only dream of such an environment. These people are the potential supporting outsider-insiders whom senior executives so desperately need to help transform organizations.

Unfortunately, many organizations turn to a true outsider, like an external consultant, to facilitate the introduction of new ideas. This is extremely aggravating for outsider-insiders, especially when they hear their own ideas being parroted back by outsiders who are being paid for their supposedly fresh ideas. It's even worse when these outsider-insiders aren't even asked for their ideas but are the ones who have to implement those that are pushed on them by outsiders who may not fully appreciate the intricacies of their work unit. As one young engineer lamented,

> We're really trying to improve cycle time. Most of the problems and resistance to change are cultural between the various functions and parts of the company. Although I could have suggested a process to reduce cycle times, they hired a consulting group to take the necessary steps. It is interesting to see how this works. Basically, these consultants only deal with the top people. Once they have the approval from the top, they just go to the relevant parts of the organization and make changes in whichever way they want without dealing with those involved in the actual processes directly. . . . I don't get the attention like these consultants do to make changes.

The situation facing this frustrated individual epitomizes the world in which many outsider-insiders find themselves. Although most organizations say they want change, outsider-insiders typically encounter enormous organizational resistance to their new ideas and perspectives. The path to successfully introducing new ideas is far from easy, and many proponents of change opt out along the way. Outsider-insiders who are successful in introducing new ideas or innovations have to prod, tweak, nudge, and sometimes shock their organizations. A common thread among the successful ones is an understanding of their respective organizational and work group cultures and an ability to find cracks in their proud, entrenched organizations to start the ball rolling. But finding opportunities that will pull in change is far from a solo act. It's a joint effort that requires patience and skills on the part of the outsider-insiders, coupled with organizational support that nurtures outsider perspectives.

Both individuals and their organizations must acknowledge the need to work together; this is a two-way street. Outsider-insiders must appreciate that true change is hard work, and opportunities to do so are rarely delivered on a silver platter. Similarly, organizations that expect outsider-insiders to single-handedly implement new ideas are living in their own fantasy world. For individuals, this means working within the existing culture and finding opportunities where they can use their unique perspectives to help solve key organizational challenges. The flip side is that organizations must learn to value outsider perspectives and create support systems that help outsider-insiders navigate through the tumultuous waters of pulling change into large and complex enterprises.

Developing a Cadre of Outsider-Insiders

Although many senior executives recognize the value of outsider-insiders, they need to do more than just click their fingers or throw pixie dust across the organization to convince others that these folks are valuable assets who need to be nurtured and rewarded. And they have to stop dreaming that simply hiring in will be the all-purpose solution. They must consciously develop and execute a strategy to develop and support a cadre of outsider-insiders throughout their organization.

There are two types of outsider-insiders: outsiders who become socialized as an insider but retain their ability to step back and look at their situation as an outsider, and insiders who learn to take an outsider perspective. Hence, organizations that want to build a critical mass of outsider-insiders need both to help insiders learn how to question assumptions and facilitate an accelerated credibility-building process for newly recruited outsiders. This does not imply, in any way, that outsider-insiders should be treated with kid gloves or treated as "special people." They merely possess a competency that is as critical and valuable as unique technical skills and should be developed and managed, as are technical experts.

Many organizations assume that the easiest way to create outsider-insiders is to hire new employees and assimilate them into the culture. The assimilation process, however, is what often destroys outsider perspectives. Thus, the socialization process for new entries must help them quickly learn about the organizational culture without stripping away their outsider hat and jump-start building an internal network to aid in finding opportunities to apply their "fresh" perspectives. The new recruits must also find ways to maintain external links and remain inquisitive as they build credibility and become part of the organization.

Becoming an outsider-insider from within (as opposed to a new employee) can start by recognizing a challenge that causes the insider to question internal assumptions or through being exposed to alternative perspectives that forces an examination of existing assumptions, as shown in Figure 1.1. It really doesn't matter which of these triggers comes first, but both are necessary for ultimately seeing opportunities to pull in change.

For their part, insiders, who have already been assimilated into an organization, can pick up outsider views in a number of ways. They may have a natural curiosity and maintain a diverse network of friends and work associates. These networks help them to continually question their own assumptions and those of their organizations. Or they may work with an external consultant, read a book, or listen to an inspirational speaker who leads them to question their fundamental assumptions about the world they live and work in. Another way that outsider-insiders are potentially created is through development activities, for example, going back to school or taking a new assignment in a vastly different part of the organization (such as a new function or location). Development activities are a way to break individuals out of any ingrained mental models that tend to foster complacency and reject diverse points of view. Overall, being an outsider-insider means creating and maintaining an attitude that continuously questions underlying assumptions. This is a process that can and should be managed.

Figure 1.1. The Development of Outsider-Insiders

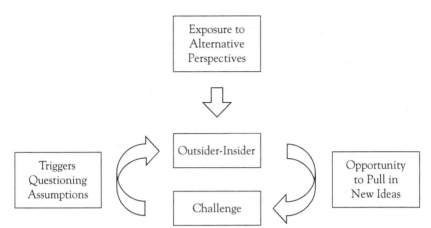

Although some people may be more predisposed to becoming an outsider-insider, it is a learned behavior. When people become socialized and assimilated into one way of thinking, they need a jolt to question their assumptions. That jolt usually comes in the form of some sort of life experience that provokes an examination of what they believe to be true, such as a test or trial or a crucible.[9] This often happens to individuals who have lived their entire lives in one locality and are sent on overseas assignments. They find an environment that is so radically different from what they are accustomed to that they begin questioning their assumptions about everything—both at work and outside work. The point is that overcoming adversity forces insiders to question their theories about why things work as they do and opens the door for them to become outsider-insiders. Sometimes jolts are totally nonwork related, but many are things that either managers or individuals can influence or control.

Being an outsider-insider can be situational. Many people are one-shot outsider-insiders. They may have even been successful in introducing a new concept but revert back to their traditional ways of thinking once the immediate challenge is conquered. These momentary outsider-insiders quickly get reassimilated into the culture. Others learn to be outsider-insiders at an early age, and this attitude stays with them throughout their lifetime. The differentiating factor is whether they learn from the experience and recognize that it was their assumptions that were the root cause of their problem in the first place. Once they internalize that lesson, they are well on their way to being perpetual outsider-insiders: people who are able to avoid looking at situations through cultural blinders.

Although some individuals are outsider-insiders by nature, most people require help in learning how to wear two hats. Even those outsider-insiders who look at their world as an outsider need assistance in how to use their multiple perspectives effectively. Few organizational cultures are friendly to unconventional thinkers. So organizations that want to nurture outsider-insiders need to build support systems that attract and develop employees who can translate their ideas into organizational improvements.

Building a Change Capability into an Organization

There is a natural tendency to look for a magic bullet or a prescriptive approach to solve the eternal question of how to lead a change effort. Unfortunately, true change doesn't happen that way. As you read this book, you will not find any quick answers. True change takes time; it is not a simple quick fix where you bring in the change agents and straighten out the organization. It is the systematic creation of a change capability through learning how to build and use outsider-insider expertise.

This book is divided into two parts. The first part (Chapters Two through Four) lays down the foundation for true change, and the second (Chapters Five through Eight) walks through the process for building and maintaining a critical mass of outsider-insiders. Throughout the chapters, your will hear the stories of our interviewees, often in their own words. The imagery in their comments was rich and vivid, and I have chosen to use their quotations to ground the theory of true change in reality.

Our journey begins with a deeper look at how cultural blinders lead to missed signals, reading the wrong signals, flawed analyses, and application of wrong solutions. As we have seen, outsider-insiders are in a position to observe these errors, but they must turn them into opportunities to pull in their outsider perspectives. The pull-change framework in Chapter Two provides a process that maximizes the probability that outsider perspectives will lead to successful implementation of new ideas and true change.

Organizations have myriad challenges, however. Some of those need more immediate attention than others, and outsider-insiders need guidance as to which ones they should attack first. So in Chapter Three, we examine the alignment of daily micro challenges with macro environmental and competitive challenges. The chapter describes how outsider-insiders must focus on working-level challenges that are barriers to achieving strategic and tactical objectives. But there is a danger that ideas pulled in on a local basis are only piecemeal changes. Hence, this chapter also outlines how outsider-insiders at the top, middle, and lower levels of an organization must work in unison to propagate new ideas throughout the organization to create true change.

A critical point throughout this book is that "the culture" is not "the enemy": it is something to be worked with and leveraged. Over time, the effect of multiple pulls will change a culture, but when change is first pulled, it is pulled into something existing— that is, the current culture. Building on our study of twelve major corporations, Chapter Four investigates ways that outsider-insiders can use the existing culture to begin getting others to recognize alternative perspectives. As we will see, three structural beams can provide leverage for outsider-insiders: (1) the criteria that organizations use to evaluate ideas, (2) whom organizational members listen to, and (3) whether outsider perspectives need authorization by influential champions.

The second half of the book turns to building an organizational capability for true change. The architecture for building that capability is infrastructure that aids outsider-insiders as they go about finding opportunities to pull change into their organizations. The infrastructure is a set of interdependent practices and policies that helps insiders develop outside perspectives and nurture new recruits as they become outsider-insiders. Developing and effectively using a cadre of outsider-insiders is not just hiring creative people or sending insiders off to a training program to be exposed to new ideas. And it is not a responsibility simply handed off to the human resource department. Rather, creating an outsider-insider support infrastructure is the work of line managers who are themselves outsider-insiders and see the need for creating a critical mass of outsider-insiders at the working level who are aligned with the macro challenges.

Building on the idea that one must leverage the existing culture to change it, we will use two best practices cases to illustrate the need to develop outsider-insider support systems that fit into (but nudge) the current organizational culture. We will compare and contrast two large corporations that have consciously attempted to develop and nurture outsider-insiders. Each developed an infrastructure that fit its unique cultural attributes. BigFab, a traditionally risk-averse fabrication and assembly operation, built formal systems that leveraged its hierarchical, top-down culture. HiTech had to rely on a more informal approach using internal networks, since its meritocratic policies dictated that no group be afforded special development opportunities. In the end, both were successful in building a critical mass of outsider-insiders to help their respective organizations respond to changing competitive environments.[10]

As we have noted, there are two sources of raw materials for developing perpetual two-hatters: outsiders and insiders. Down the road, they look the same as both become outsider-insiders. But insiders need to be exposed to outside ideas and learn how to wear two hats, and outsiders need to develop credibility as an insider without losing their ability to see things through an outsider's hat. Hence, the processes for developing these two groups into outsider-insiders are quite different but need to be symbiotic. As shown in

Figure 1.2, the two paths merge and become one once people learn how to wear two hats: that's the point where the two sources look the same.

In Chapter Five, we explore two routes by which insiders become outsider-insiders. The first is through immersion on the outside (for example, cross-functional or overseas assignments or going back to school full-time). But organizations often do not have the time or the resources to provide large groups of employees with such development opportunities. Hence, the second route is by looking through a window to the outside (for example, being a member of an interdisciplinary or globally dispersed team or attending classes on a part-time basis). Although cultural blinders, or what we will call cobwebs on the window, tend to restrict what insiders see when they look to the outside, there are processes to help insiders clear away those strands.

Figure 1.2. Building Organizational Capability for True Change

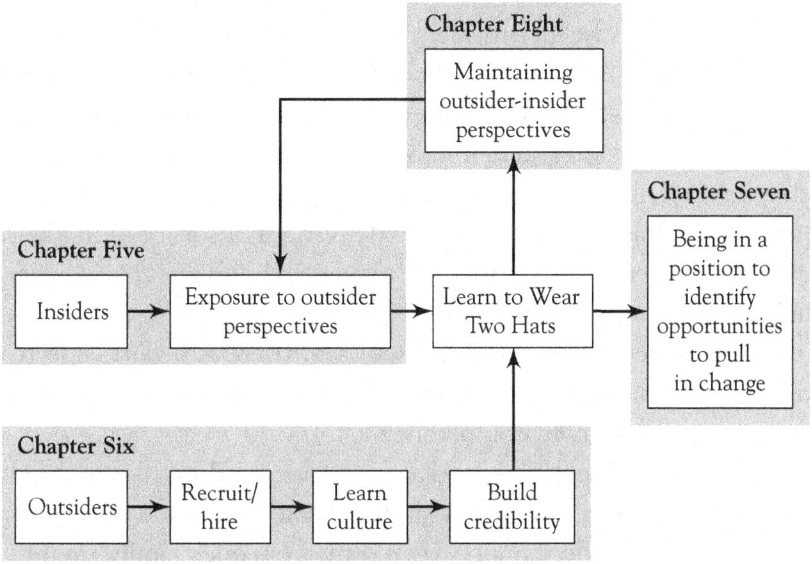

Note: Champions, mentors, and networks are critical at each step.

We then move to bringing in outsiders and teaching them how to wear two hats—in other words, encouraging them to continually address challenges with fresh perspectives the way they will do during their first few months in an organization. As Chapter Six makes clear, this is no small feat. There must be truth in advertising on both sides—by the potential newcomer and the organization—to avoid unrealistic expectations. Organizations must clearly articulate their current and aspired cultures, and individuals must be honest around their personal goals and objectives and the type of organization they feel comfortable working in. Once outsiders are on the inside, they must learn the culture and build credibility as an insider without losing their outsider perspectives; that is, they must become integrated without being totally assimilated.

Creating a critical mass of outsider-insiders is only the first half of building an organizational capability for true change. Outsider-insiders are always in a state of potential; pulling change is the outcome of tapping into that potential. Unfortunately, many opportunities to pull in new ideas end up being merely serendipitous without a system that consciously matches outsider-insiders to key organizational challenges. Chapter Seven begins with the story of a senior-level outsider-insider who is a self-proclaimed "network attractor," that is, a person who has a large network and uses it to help other outsider-insiders get to the right place at the right time to identify gaps and help solve organizational challenges. The chapter describes how networks are built and used to implement new ideas. One critical network node is the sponsors of individual outsider-insiders who act as matchmakers to help outsider-insiders find key challenges that will provide opportunities for pulling in outside perspectives. But as we will see, there is a dark side to heavy-handed advocacy, and at some point outsider-insiders must demonstrate their own competence.

Outsider-insiders also need a support network of like-minded folks. These people provide a sounding board and coach or mentor fellow outsider-insiders. Support can come from one's family, friends, or work environment, but our focus is on the last of these. Mentors play a critical role in helping outsider-insiders to exploit opportunities to pull in change. Sometimes one mentor serves multiple roles, but most outsider-insiders develop a network of mentors. These mentors or coaches provide support, formal and informal, for developing and sustaining people who are often viewed as, and treated like, aliens within their organizations. Furthermore, support networks help to diffuse outsider perspectives and build a critical mass of outsider-insiders who are ready and able to use their two hats to find opportunities to pull in new ideas in response to environmental or macro pulls. But at every step of the way, the outsider-insider "supply chain" is a shared responsibility between outsider-insiders and their organizations. Opportunities are not just given to developing outsider-insiders; they must be earned.

But no matter how good the support system may be, outsider-insiders who attempt to pull change have to fight against losing their ability to continually reevaluate current assumptions. It is a constant struggle to keep the two hats in balance. Some people gravitate toward insider ways of thinking, while others clinch so tightly to their outsider hat that they lose credibility as an insider. With few organizations truly valuing countercultural points of view, outsider-insiders must possess perseverance to simultaneously wear both hats and continually examine assumptions—their organization's and their own. Without continual vigilance, individuals can find themselves in the same rut as their organization: stuck in their own set of assumptions that prevent them from accepting alternative points of view.

We conclude the book with a look at how outsider-insiders can, and must, continually examine their own assumptions to prevent getting caught in the vicious cycle they are trying to break. As they encounter new situations, their assumptions need to evolve. When outsider-insiders are effective in getting insiders to accept outsider approaches and the resultant changes become embedded in the culture, they become just another insider unless they constantly refresh their outsider perspectives. Their value as outsider-insiders lies in their ability to repeatedly observe gaps where internal assumptions are blocking achievement of goals and objectives in a dynamic environment. Organizations can help in this regard by providing further development activities to help outsider-insiders maintain their ability to wear two hats through their careers. As we will see, true change is dynamic, and so are the careers of the people who facilitate true change.

Chapter Two

The Process of Pulling Change

Imagine a clear, sunny day with a gentle breeze blowing offshore. It is perfect weather for a sail. Usually Tom would just motor out the channel to the sea, but today he can't resist the temptation to put up the sails and let nature do the work. As he raises the sails, the breeze catches, bellowing them out. He waves to a fisherman anchored nearby and asks if he has caught anything. The fisherman shouts back, "Not much luck today." Suddenly there is a panicked look on the fisherman's face. He yells to his wife, "Mabel, Mabel, the anchor's dragging us out to sea! We're moving ahead of that sailboat!" She immediately pulls on the anchor and replies, "Seems to be holding." Tom smiles and looks up at his sails and thinks, "What a glorious day. Boy, am I glad I'm not that guy." He didn't know why the fishing boat was moving faster than he was, but that really wasn't his problem. At this point, everything seemed to be going fine from Tom's perspective.

Tom's sailing companion, Ginger, is also watching the scene in the fishing boat, amused by the commotion—that is, until she glances at the houses along the channel. She suddenly realizes that it's not the fisherman's boat that is moving forward; it's the sailboat that is actually *sailing backward*. In reality, the wind in the sails was insufficient power to overcome the strong incoming tide. At that moment, she became an outsider-insider. She saw a gap between the root cause of the situation and the prior assumption that Tom, she, and the fisherman had held: that the sails were moving the sailboat forward. Tom just kept looking forward, thinking everything was fine. Had an outsider been standing onshore, he too would have immediately seen what was happening, but the two insiders in this story, Tom and the fisherman, were both caught up in their own assumptions. Tom was thinking that he was sailing forward, and the fisherman assumed his anchor was dragging him forward. Both assumptions were logical based on experience, but they didn't reflect the reality of the situation.

A far-fetched story? It actually happened, and in retrospect, it's rather humorous. But think of the parallels that occur within organizations: when the competitive environment shifts, for example, the tides change. Many companies assume they are in great shape "going forward": customers are happy, revenue streams in, and so forth. But suddenly they find themselves "going backward." Insiders miss the signals that are often totally apparent to outsiders. It was fairly easy for Ginger to convince Tom that he had better change his strategy and turn on the engine to avoid a catastrophe. All she had to do was have him look at the shoreline to see that he was moving backward. But in many situations, insiders need more than having the problem pointed out to them. Just looking externally is not enough. After all, Tom was looking externally, but his view was too narrow and he was reading the wrong signals.

When a challenge escalates in importance and urgency, someone usually suggests an alternative practice as a potential solution to overcome the problem. In many respects, this is a pushcart approach to the introduction of alternative approaches to solve the problem. Insiders rarely step back and question their view of what the problem really is. Occasionally, the alternative suggestion actually addresses the source of the problem, but more often than not, the alternative is merely a short-term fix that masks the root cause of the problem. The result is constant firefighting to battle a series of symptoms. This random target practice to see which new idea will work leads to haphazard and frustrating change efforts. In this chapter, we shall see that the process of pulling change requires more than a challenge and a pushcart full of alternative practices; it also requires understanding how internal assumptions are getting in the way of seeing and solving a key challenge or problem.

The first step in the pulling change process is being able to step back and look for gaps between the current view of a challenge and the root cause of that challenge. This gap may not be readily apparent, but astute outsider-insiders are able to use their two hats to discern quickly why current practices or processes are not addressing the source of the problem. In Ginger's case, she was able to see that Tom's use of his sails rather than his engine was an inappropriate choice of alternative practices given the tides. She was also able to quickly observe the gap in assumptions: Tom assumed the sails would move the boat forward, but in reality the tides were moving the boat backward. As shown in Figure 2.1, it was the gap that led her to pull in the right set of alternative practices, that is, turning on the engine, to address the root cause of the challenge.

Once a gap is acknowledged, an alternative set of practices can be identified to resolve the challenge. But before insiders will consider those alternatives, they must be convinced that their current practices, which stem from their view of the problem, are what are at fault. Only then will they be open to considering an alternative approach. Granted, they may be willing to try something different on a trial or short-term basis but will quickly revert to conventional ways of doing things unless they truly understand the need for the change. This is what true change is all about: a change in mental models.

Figure 2.1. Challenges That Create Opportunities for Pulling in Outsider Perspectives

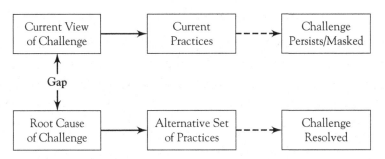

It is very easy for insiders to get tunnel vision. Time is a precious commodity in most organizations. As competitive pressures lead to a thinning of the ranks, there is never enough time to accomplish all the tasks facing employees. The result is a continual hunt for shortcuts or the most expedient way to get things done. There is little time to step back and reflect on why or how people do the things they do. Outsider-insiders are under the same time pressures and often end up just going with the flow even when they see that the expedient remedies will be only a temporary fix. If they see an imminent crisis, the hope is that they will speak up. But most of the time, they shake their heads at what appears to them as obvious inefficiencies yet feel unempowered to introduce their views. After all, the energy and time associated with voicing an alternative perspective will most likely be rebuffed by peers and managers as only getting in the way of meeting a near-term deadline.

So just because outsider-insiders see a different perspective does not necessarily mean they will automatically be proactive in trying to implement alternative ideas or concepts. Some might choose to go about their business recognizing that they see the world through a different lens. They may be frustrated and complain that others just do not "get it," but they do not necessarily become proactive simply because they see a connection that others do not. But should they decide to take the leap to being a proactive outsider-insider, it is critical that they have a clear understanding of the underlying organizational assumptions that exist and potentially work against their ability to get others to accept their outsider views.

Why We Do What We Do

The most admired companies typically have strong organizational cultures. Those cultures are what align the organization and help employees efficiently make daily decisions. Consider the HP Way. It was viewed as such a valuable asset as HP split into two companies that Carly Fiorina, HP's first outsider CEO, went to great lengths to emphasize that the basic principles that constituted the HP Way—for example, management by walking around and the open-door policy—set forth by Bill Hewlett and Dave Packard in the 1940s were still the basis for the new HP.

Cultures are made up of a set of underlying assumptions about how organizational members are expected to behave.[1] Those basic assumptions shape the world that employees see and help them to interpret events and challenges. Culture also influences how people approach challenges, what data they observe, how they analyze those data, and the options they ultimately choose to address those challenges. In other words, cultural assumptions drive behavior.

When our observations, analyses, and approaches to meeting challenges result in successfully solving problems or reaching our objectives, we tend to incorporate that sequence of events or activities into our procedures and routines. These practices can be both formal policies or operating guidelines and informal work routines. Over time, these rituals eventually become ingrained in our assumptions, and insiders tend to follow them without thinking. As shown in Figure 2.2, the result is an unconscious and unquestioned closed-loop cycle. Hence, what we see and how we see it is not only a result of our worldviews but also the basis for shaping our cultural assumptions. This is how culture becomes a reinforcing mechanism in helping an organization continue to do the things it does well.

Although this reinforcing cycle often plays itself out at an individual level, it also occurs within groups, across an organization, and even at a national level. For purposes of this book, we are primarily looking at the culture of a work unit that is facing a particular challenge. That might be a work group, a manufacturing plant or office, or an entire division of a large corporation. Since that unit is embedded within a larger culture, that of the corporation, we can never ignore the other levels because that umbrella culture affects how work units within it develop and transform their own environments over time. In Chapter Four, we explore how that larger culture can be used to leverage the introduction of new ideas and concepts.

Figure 2.2. Building Cultural Assumptions

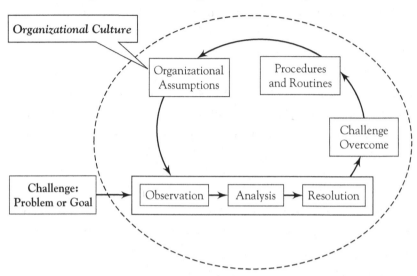

When Cultural Assumptions Fail Us

Cultural assumptions tend to co-opt our thinking. They can be so strong that they can override what appears to be logical because they influence the data we see. Such assumptions can cause us to get so ingrained in routines that we miss key signals and simply apply legacy solutions without thinking. This was brought vividly home by the *Columbia* shuttle disaster. NASA managers and engineers appeared to discount obvious danger signals that threatened the shuttle's viability. They saw the foam hit the wing and because shuttles came back safely before after having foam fly off, they assumed it was not a life-threatening situation. The NASA culture was so strong that even when individuals asked repeatedly about the foam, assurances were given that everything was fine.[2] As a result, those assumptions themselves became the root of the problem. Obviously, breaking through such routines is not easy, but it is the key to getting others to want to change the way they do things.

Socialization processes can easily keep people from being able to step back and be objective about why they do what they do.

New employees who are schooled in a company's standard operating procedures soon assume that is the way the world works, particularly if they are entering the workforce on their first job. It is very difficult to recognize that it is one's own existing paradigms that are part of the problem. Failures can occur at multiple points in the process of analyzing and attempting to solve a challenge. We identify several errors that can occur in the three-stage problem-solving process depicted in Figure 2.2:

- *Observation: Missed signals.* Andy Grove coined the phrase, "Only the Paranoid Survive," after observing one high-technology company after another missing key signals that its products were being leapfrogged by a new generation of technology. Thus, famously, the makers of mainframes and minicomputers did not see the potential of the personal computer due to a belief that PCs were just a toy and would never become powerful enough to steal market share away from the larger computers. In many respects, this was organizational arrogance, a typical artifact of cultural blinders. People were so sure of themselves and their products that they couldn't imagine that anyone could come up with a better idea. Furthermore, they were not trained and conditioned to look for potential predators.
- *Observation: Reading signals incorrectly.* There are times when warning signals are read but interpreted through the wrong lens. Tom was clearly a case in point when he neglected to look at the shoreline and subsequently didn't realize he was sailing backward. Cross-functional problems often fall into this category. The dominant function, for example, the most powerful one with the most organizational status or clout, may influence what signals are received and analyzed. In Tom's case, his sailboat was clearly larger than the small fishing boat. As a result, the fisherman initially assumed the problem was with his boat rather than the dominant, much larger sailboat.

Part of the problem is time. Someone who is in the middle of wrestling with a challenge tends to look for obvious causes and solutions. The need for speed leads one to fall back on what one knows or has tried in the past. Taking the time to find additional data or double-check to make sure that the data are correct is often viewed as analysis paralysis.

- *Analysis: Flawed reasoning.* There are other times when problems are recognized and the symptoms are self-evident, but our analysis is flawed. Once again, the fisherman is a case in point since his first analysis was that his anchor was somehow dragging him forward. His error was much easier to see than the dilemma facing American manufacturers in the mid-1980s. Their problem was evident: a loss of market share due to a major competitive challenge from Japanese producers. But diagnosing the problem was far more difficult. Rather than just getting better at what American producers were already doing, in other words, throwing more technical wizardry at the problem, they needed to step back and reexamine their base assumptions about manufacturing. Unfortunately, most U.S. managers and academics assumed the problem could be solved by technology. That's what competitive challenges were all about, they believed. What they missed was that Japanese manufacturers were working against a very different set of product and process assumptions.

While Americans pursued economies of scale achieved through better technology, the Japanese recognized the need for flexibility and superior quality. At an operational level, American manufacturers created huge, capital-intensive factories with equipment dedicated to specific products. This made factory layouts difficult and expensive to change. The Japanese came up with a strategy to produce mixed models on the same assembly line. They also put machines on wheels with connections dropping from the ceiling. In short, they had found a way to make their operations lean not because of technology itself but as a consequence of how they used the technology. They also started using statistical analyses (statistical process control, SPC) to reduce product defects at the plant floor. As one outsider-insider within one of the North American manufacturers we studied recalled,

The company has a history of looking for a silver bullet. It has the reputation of having a program of the month—in the early '80s it was SPC, but that's now gone. We then wanted to be like Toyota. We saw that they used *kanban*, pull system, JIT [just-in-time]; so we said let's implement it. We spent billions of dollars but it doesn't work, because we cherry-picked. We don't look at things as a system. We don't look deep enough and see what they really do.

The difference this individual identified was more than just tools and techniques; it was an integrated way of thinking and managing a total system or enterprise. The typical domestic approach was to find the pushcarts that rolled most easily rather than looking for the root cause of the problem and finding the solution that would address that problem.

- *Resolution: Applying the wrong solution.* Narrow tunnel vision can also lead to selecting a faulty solution. We continue to live with the QWERTY keyboard because mechanical typewriters kept jamming when secretaries typed faster than the early machines were designed to function. The designers assumed that they could not create a machine to keep up with the typists, so they jumbled the keyboard to slow the typists down. Even after machines became fast, no one changed the keyboard since thousands of people had already learned to type with the jumbled keyboard.

  Even when the appropriate signs are observed and the analysis is right on target, the chosen solution can fall short. Intel's reaction to its well-publicized Pentium flaw is a perfect example. Their engineers did a sound analysis of the likelihood of the flaw's causing a problem for anyone other than researchers doing heavy-duty statistical analysis and concluded that the flaw would not be a problem for the vast number of general computer operators. Their analysis was most likely correct, but they missed the point. They were thinking like engineers (after all, Intel is an engineering company) and assumed that clear logic would rule the day. But it didn't with the general public, which didn't understand the company's technical analysis. The general public didn't want to buy computers powered by chips that made mistakes.

Past successes can also blind people to alternative solutions. The current approach may not be bad or wrong, but it may not be as good as it might be if the culture is open to different perspectives. As one thoughtful outsider-insider in a very successful company observed,

> There is a feeling that we are the best. It can be a hindrance to learning. . . . When we work with an equipment vendor, it is easy to assume that their practices are backward or Neanderthal but they may be appropriate for their industry. Our process may be two or three times more expensive and we are blind to learning what is different in their industry. We lean toward perfectionism and accept that premium quality is worth the cost of over specifying.

All of these examples appear self-evident in retrospect. Furthermore, observing a gap and doing something about it are two different things. As we will see, getting others to understand their blind spots requires a great deal of finesse on the part of outsider-insiders. All too often, outsider-insiders become frustrated when their managers and peers do not see what they see: that their cultural assumptions are blocking progress. In fact, many insiders may not even recognize that they have a problem because existing metrics can easily mask issues. This may likely have been the case in Tom's sailing escapade. His metric was sails bellowing out. His goal was a leisurely sail. Distance traveled or a timely arrival at a predetermined destination was not something he was paying attention to. It took Ginger to see the fallacy in his assumptions. Her role, as with most other outsider-insiders, was to help Tom to see that he had a problem.

But talking in broad generalities about the problems with current cultural assumptions usually falls on deaf ears. If the fisherman had not noticed that something was wrong and Ginger had just started explaining to Tom how strong incoming tides can be, it would have been just a philosophical discussion. Tom may never have connected the concept to his situation. In other words, presenting new ideas just for the sake of doing something different goes nowhere. As one proactive outsider-insider put it, "Everyone seemed open to new ideas, everyone was looking for new and different ways to do things, but when you suggested something, their reaction was 'I could never make that kind of change.'" What this outsider-insider himself failed to see was that pulling change requires finding the right place and the right time to introduce alternative perspectives and then linking those perspectives to important and urgent challenges.

A Framework for Pulling Change

Ideas alone are merely academic exercises; it is an unattainable or unsolved challenge that creates a pull for new ideas. As one technical manager who was responsible for disseminating best practices across his organization recognized, "A technical summary report will not work. It really takes someone walking into my office and saying, 'I have a problem,' and we say, 'I think I might have a solution for you.'" As this comment implies, the process of pulling change begins with identifying a challenge where cultural assumptions are getting in the way of either solving a problem or meeting an objective.

For managers, challenges can be problematic, but to outsider-insiders, they are uncut stones waiting to be polished into precious gems. Just as a diamond cutter examines rough stones for brilliant

facets, outsider-insiders look for gaps between root causes of a challenge and their organization's assumptions as to what the challenge
is and the best way to approach it. These gaps are opportunities to
pull new ideas into the organization. The initial idea for Intel's leg-
endary Copy Exactly concept stemmed from one of those opportunities. Back in the early 1990s, there were yield gaps between the
development facility and the manufacturing operations. Each
facility was doing its own thing to close the gap, but the gap kept
getting worse. This was at a time when the market was mush-
rooming and the semiconductor industry had a massive shortage
in capacity.

The yield gap, coupled with the capacity shortfall, provided
the initial pull for the Copy Exactly concept. When the Pentium
was introduced, one of the plant managers decided to copy
the equipment and the physical layout that was being used in the
development facility. While the idea of learning from other facilities and copying best practices was common, copying things to this
extent was not. Hence, at that moment, the plant manager became
a proactive outsider-insider. He may not have consciously recognized that his idea was very similar to standardized work processes
that are a cornerstone in lean manufacturing systems, but the
general approach of copying another operation was an idea on
the outside of the organization.

After the Pentium ramp-up in his facility was a success, the
manager shared his idea with his peers within the plant manager
network. Another plant manager decided to pick up the idea
(pulled it in to help solve challenges within his facility) and used it
to the extreme, copying not only equipment but all production
processes. The concept worked so well that it quickly became a
mandate from the executive team, and a third plant quickly signed
up to implement Copy Exactly. The fourth plant was reluctant and
decided to introduce its own reengineering program instead of
Copy Exactly. But its program failed to narrow the gap, which further demonstrated the power of Copy Exactly. Eventually, after the

pressure to improve yields at the fourth plant mounted (another challenge to pull in the idea), the reluctant manager agreed to introduce Copy Exactly.

It was the persistence of the capacity and yield challenge that set the stage for pulling in the idea of Copy Exactly. As the capacity shortfall mounted, it became evident that something needed to change; there was a challenge that cultural assumptions could not solve. This opened the door for the Copy Exactly concept. It worked so well that it became a formal part of the management reviews, that is, a corporate initiative. Over time, the new behaviors engendered by Copy Exactly transformed the plant's assumptions about appropriate processes for introducing innovation within the operation. In other words, Copy Exactly became institutionalized: true change had occurred.

Figure 2.3 illustrates the process for pulling change as seen in the Copy Exactly illustration. The following paragraphs describe the elements needed for new ideas or change to be pulled in.

Figure 2.3. The Process of Pulling Change

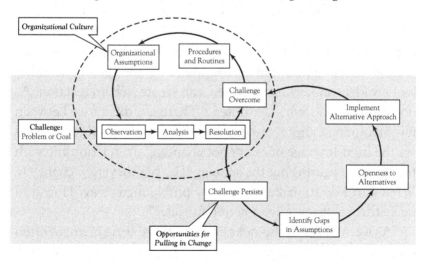

Identifying Opportunities to Pull in Change

Organizations have many challenges, and the key is in finding the right ones that will begin the move toward true change. The proactive outsider-insider has an eye for challenges that are both urgent and important. These are the challenges that provide the opportunity to question cultural assumptions. Being urgent without being important, or vice versa, is not enough to capture attention. It is way too easy to procrastinate on even important problems. Take dieting as an example. Most people know that excess weight is dangerous to their health. There is no question that it is an important issue, but it usually takes something more urgent, such as clothes that no longer fit or a pressing health problem, to get people to begin changing their eating habits, including passing dessert. Similarly, no one at Intel, a company built on a deeply entrenched engineering culture that prides itself on innovation, would have considered copying someone else's design if there hadn't been an overwhelming challenge that was getting more and more critical.

Most organizations have hundreds of urgent challenges that unfortunately trigger only firefighting actions. But at some point, an organization runs out of firefighting resources, and the challenge finally becomes *the* important one. Sometimes challenges are systemic, such as the capacity shortfall within the semiconductor industry, but often the challenge is just a daily problem that is both important and urgent to the people involved. Small changes are the low-hanging fruit that create small wins that build credibility for new ideas and, when corrected, can create a chain reaction. As one astute outsider-insider noted, "There is a difference between revolutionizing things versus making little changes. The little changes are the high-leverage ones. It's not changing the relationship with the union or figuring out the strategy. The high-leverage change is, What can I do to make the quality problem go away? How do I make this employee have a better attitude?"

As we will see in the next chapter, these little changes often propagate and help address more strategic issues. This, of course, requires an alignment between the micro-level problems and more strategic macro challenges. Regardless of the perceived size of the problem, true change requires some form of behavioral change; the challenge must require more than just a technical fix. Getting others to routinely change their behavior, no matter how minor that change may be, requires reexamining and altering the work group's mental models relative to the challenge at hand. It demands adaptive change rather than a mere technical fix.[3]

The introduction of lean manufacturing principles is a prime example. Many adopters assumed that lean manufacturing merely means reducing inventory or rearranging a factory floor into production cells. That's the artifact, or technical-physical change, they see when they visit a lean operation. But beneath the surface is a key set of underlying process assumptions that are clearly different than in a mass production environment. Mass production works on the principle of economies of scale so that costs can be spread over higher and higher volumes. Lean producers, for their part, assume that any non-value-added activity is waste, no matter what the volume might be. The latter requires an immense degree of discipline by the entire organization that is typically not found in traditional mass production operations. Hence, moving to lean requires a technical solution (such as inventory reduction), a cultural change (underlying assumptions concerning waste), and a behavioral modification (discipline). But individuals trying to introduce lean practices can talk until they are blue in the face about discipline. It is not something that most people are able to imagine. To get people to see the value of discipline, there must be a challenge within a specific work area that illustrates that work-arounds are the root cause of the group's inability to reach a performance target. That challenge—an inability to meet performance goals—is the opportunity for an outsider-insider to begin the process of questioning assumptions as to why employees use work-arounds and introducing the idea of discipline as an alternative approach to daily operations.

Helping Insiders Identify Gaps in Assumptions

As many concerned friends or family members who want to help an addict change behavior know all too well, it is only when the addicts themselves recognize their problem that their recovery can begin. The same is true for organizations. This is the reason that so many consultants have an easy time convincing managers to try new methods: they typically get called in to fix a problem only after it has become both urgent and important. But all too often, the challenges that outsider-insiders see are not observable to their managers, peers, and subordinates. In these cases, the outsider-insider's role is to help others to see the failure of their paradigms for themselves. This often involves finding just the right moment to raise a question and engage insiders in a dialogue about why people do things the way they do. One of the easiest ways is asking questions and gathering data. One outsider-insider noted, "The value of an outside perspective comes from asking questions. When insiders answer the questions, they learn. It is like when children ask you *why, why, why*. You have to think about things and figure them out."

Alternatively, outsider-insiders can help others see the gaps by showing them what their current assumptions are costing them. But outsider-insiders must do more than just announce there is a problem pending. They must show that the cost of continuing to do things as they always have is greater than changing.[4] In technocratic organizations, a sound analysis may be all that is necessary. But as we will see in Chapter Four, logic alone will be insufficient in experience-based cultures. In this case, outsider-insiders will have to focus their attention on veterans who can be their allies in helping others to question their assumptions.

Helping insiders to see their blind spots typically requires enormous patience and one-on-one hand-holding. As one outsider-insider observed, "It takes time to motivate people, to make them want to change." And another noted that it has to be done in a way that alleviates any fears that insiders may hold: "I find myself spending a lot of time in one-on-one meetings with people. It takes a lot of time. I try to find out what they believe in and what is at the root of their fears. I find it is almost always fear based. Then I help them trace back to something that happened in the past and try to show how this time, things are different."

In other words, the role of the outsider-insider is to get others to begin questioning their assumptions as to the root cause of the challenge and why they are approaching the problem as they currently are. It is important to reiterate that the outsider-insider is not the agent of change; it is the challenge that pulls in new ideas. At this point in the pulling change framework, the focus remains on the challenge, not the new idea that is about to be pulled in to address the challenge. A veteran outsider-insider whose career was built on repeatedly helping insiders see the gaps in their thinking instructed:

> If you go in and say, "Holy cow, look at the dead body on the floor. Who killed it?" no one else sees it. You have to make sure others don't fear the gap. There may be legitimate reasons why the gap exists and you need to listen to insiders to understand if that is the case. It took me a while but I finally came to understand what vision is all about—it's about helping people to see the gap and have different perspectives. But they can't be threatened. You can't hit them over the head and tell them how stupid they are and how screwed up things are.

Openness to Alternatives

It is only after the lightbulb has gone on, revealing that something is wrong or missing, that people become open to alternative explanations. At this point, they are aware that they need to change but are uncertain as to what that change should be. One successful proactive outsider-insider described it as helping people to "envision the future." So in addition to wearing two hats and identifying a gap in assumptions, proactive outsider-insiders must now be ready with, or help others search for, a tool kit of ideas and alternative approaches that might address the root cause of the problem that is now apparent. The presentation of these new ideas needs to be done in a way that people can see how an alternative approach will help them overcome any remaining misgivings. An outsider-insider who was trying to introduce supply chain concepts said about his colleagues, "They are so deep in their problems. They didn't feel it was truly applicable to them because they didn't want to take the time to work through the theories. I learned that giving them general theories is a waste of their time and mine. It was better to give them specifics in their language and their problem sets."

As this astute outsider-insider discovered, true change occurs only when people can visualize how alternative approaches will help them solve problems they face. That is the reason that benchmarking other organizations to identify opportunities for improvement often delivers meager results. Just imitating another organization's practices or structure does not necessarily mean there is understanding or a questioning of the assumptions held by the benchmarked organization. It is only when that benchmarking is tied to a real challenge that people are positioned to begin questioning their own mental models.

Implementation of Alternative Approaches

The pulling in of the change finally occurs when the alternative approach is applied in an effort to solve the problem. As we saw with Copy Exactly, these "new" ideas or concepts need not be inventions per se. They just need to be new to the people facing the challenge. Although the alternative approaches are typically suggested by a proactive outsider-insider, it must be the people who ultimately need to put the new ideas into practice who make the discovery for themselves.

Sometimes the need for alternative approaches is clear to everyone; at other times, it surfaces only after results are achieved. This is where an outsider-insider must methodically reframe problems to help others see how alternative approaches are worth trying out, even if on a trial basis. Looking back, a senior outsider-insider recalled the process he used to help employees in a newly acquired facility accept being part of a larger matrixed organization:

> I had to educate folks in how to work in a matrix and many of them didn't want to work that way. They hadn't worked that way, so they don't know how it works. First, I had to listen long enough to understand where folks were coming from and why they were having trouble with working in a matrix. Then I presented them with a different mental model. The site they came from was an intact operation—they managed their whole world, including marketing, working with suppliers, etc. Now they are just a cog in the wheel and part of the larger organization. I had to show them that it is a different context and then structure a model in a way that fits with what they knew and what they had done. I had to have the discussion up-front to get a common understanding. Then we just started working in the new way. After about a quarter, 90 percent of the resistance was gone; 10 percent still existed, but it was almost there.

Once insiders begin living with alternative approaches, many start to see how those new concepts might work better than their old ways of doing things.

Overcoming the Challenge

The process of pulling in a new concept or idea is complete once the immediate challenge is overcome. This now sets the stage for cementing the new ideas into the organizational culture. It is the institutionalization of the new ideas that qualifies as true change. For that to happen, the newly discovered patterns of behavior must become part of the procedures and routines, that is, embedded in the upper loop in Figure 2.3. Otherwise, it is merely a onetime, not permanent, change. One manager noted, "What are the things to ensure that this change ensures that problems will not occur? . . . There are loads of small changes which need to be done, like making sure when tools break that there is a system in place to know why and what to do so it doesn't happen again. We know how to solve symptoms, but we usually don't go back and put in a system to lessen the severity or minimize a reoccurrence of a problem."

If the challenge that was overcome was relatively small or localized to a specific unit, there may be a need to replicate the success to convince others that it is more than an isolated case and that the basis for the action and results are grounded in a different set of assumptions that require systemic change.

Rarely are an organization's support systems aligned with the new ideas that have been pulled in to address workplace issues. Success may occur at a local level, but it may have been accomplished in spite of established procedures and routines. All too often, this becomes short-term change or totally dependent on the personalities of the people directly involved with it. A misaligned infrastructure, such as metrics or information systems, typically provides excuses or points of resistance for institutionalizing the new ideas. For true change to occur, the procedures and routines, both formal and informal, must be revamped to be congruent with the new alternative approaches that have been implemented.

The introduction of participative work systems is a perfect example. In the typical scenario, a manager is dissatisfied with productivity levels and assumes that introducing self-directed work teams will boost efficiency. The workforce goes through some initial team-based training sessions that ask the supervisors to share their decision-making activities with their work groups. The promise is improved morale and a more committed workforce. After a quick boost in productivity, often a result of a halo or Hawthorne effect, problems (re)surface. Supervisors often revert to old behaviors when problems arise: things start falling through the cracks if the workforce is ill prepared to address issues that had typically been handled by the supervisors. Looking at this "regression," a likely first assumption is that the supervisors haven't made the mental model leap to the new paradigm and are eager to jump back into the fray. This may indeed be true, but more likely it is that the infrastructure (such as information systems or middle management decision-making processes) is unable to support work team decisions. Improvement occurs only when modifications are made to the infrastructure that provides information and processes to allow the workforce to truly take on greater responsibility. At that point, supervisors realize that they can start to let go, and good decisions can be made without their micromanagement. The change is therefore a redesign of the organization's procedures and systems, plus a transformation in supervisory (and workforce) behavior. Both require pulling in new cultural assumptions about how work is done and supported. Since support typically requires coordination across functions and across hierarchical levels, outsider-insiders must be aligned throughout the organization to ensure that new ideas that are being pulled in are in congruence with one another and larger organizational objectives, the subject we will turn to in the next chapter.

Applying the Pull-Change Framework

It is now clear that outsider-insiders are essential to finding opportunities to pull in new ideas or ways of doing business. As insiders, they are members of the internal community. They know the family secrets, both good and bad. They speak a language unique to the clan—a shorthand that they learned as they were socialized into "the gang." They know how to read the clues and body language. There is an unspoken understanding of what is expected of them as insiders. It is built up over time. There is trust based on history and shared understanding of roles, responsibilities, and accountabilities. It is a family. For some insiders, it can be a closed society, but not for outsider-insiders. They have the unique ability to see outside, to see the bigger picture and make connections to the world beyond the boundaries of their group—in other words, to wear two hats.

As outsider-insiders, they can provide a bridge. They have the opportunity to translate external perspectives into what works for their organizations. This works only when they are truly "in." This is not work for consultants; it is work within the organization. The legitimacy of the change is acknowledged only when it comes from within, at the grassroots level. Sometimes senior champions anoint outsider-insiders as key proponents of new ideas. Many outsider-insiders in our studies preferred this mode: anointed outsider-insiders at least have official organizational support. But being anointed in an adversarial environment can only set outsider-insiders up on a pedestal to be shot down. "We carry this big bull's eye around that says that 'I'm special,'" lamented one anointed outsider-insider at a large manufacturer. "People like nothing more than poking at something special."

For outsider-insiders, deciding whether to be proactive in helping their organization address the gaps they see is a pivotal step—sometimes conscious, but not always. Furthermore, from an organizational point of view, some outsider perspectives are more valuable than others. In fact, some may even be detrimental if they run counter to the strategic direction of the firm or may fail to understand the complexities of a particular situation (this is addressed in Chapter Three). Hence, outsider-insiders face a critical decision point: Do they actively pursue disseminating their worldview or sit quietly in the background doing the job they have been asked to do? Although this decision may appear to be a clear-cut go/no-go, it may be more a question of timing and opportunity.

Ultimately, it requires personal desire and motivation to take on organizational norms and assumptions. It also takes more than simply wearing two hats and seeing where internal assumptions are holding the organization back from being the best it can be. Lone outsider-insiders cannot do it alone. They need their organization's help in learning about and being in a position to contribute to overcoming systemic-wide challenges. They need coaching and guidance in how and where to apply the pull-change framework to increase the probability that true change will occur. As we will see in the forthcoming chapters, organizations need to help outsider-insiders in these ways:

1. See a problem or challenge where internal assumptions are getting in the way of overcoming that challenge
2. See how their outsider views can help overcome that challenge
3. Have the skills and expertise to approach the challenge from an alternative point of view
4. Have the credibility and cultural awareness to get others to accept alternative assumptions and approaches to solve their challenges

Chapter Three

Aligning Pulls Across the Organization

Having legions of outsider-insiders questioning assumptions without a common understanding of their organization's priorities can lead to chaos and disenchantment on the part of outsider-insiders; people feel no one is listening to them. More critical, the new ways of doing things that outsider-insiders introduce must be aligned with an organization's strategic and operational objectives if these ideas are to have impact, much less be transformative. As one outsider-insider recognized, "I need to know the corporate perspective so when I am back in my own piece of the world, I know what's going on. It is important not to make a decision for my unit that doesn't make sense for the corporation." Clearly, this individual understood the importance of linking local-level change to broader organizational strategies and tactics. As such, he was better able to focus his outsider hat on challenges that were important to the firm overall, not just him personally.

There are plenty of alternative ideas "out there," and many of those should probably remain out there. Furthermore, many people quickly jump on the latest trend or bandwagon simply because it is something that everyone else seems to be doing. The ideas may be good ones but may not fit with where the organization is headed. As we have seen, ideas are pulled in only by an unresolved challenge that provides an opportunity for an outsider-insider to help other insiders start to question their assumptions. But those ideas must also be related to the firm's strategic and tactical goals, not someone's pet project or new for the sake of newness.

Furthermore, when a working-level outsider-insider identifies a need for alternative ways of doing things, there is a danger that ideas that are pulled in on a local basis are only piecemeal changes that are not propagated throughout the organization. A handful of individual outsider-insiders can do only so much in large organizations. Their ability to help a significant portion of their organization to question their assumptions is minuscule. Instead, organizations need to build a critical mass of outsider-insiders all using their alternative approaches in unison to pull in systemic change. As one manager noted, "Piecemeal knowledge tends to get localized and then disappears. It is just noise in the bigger system. It is like hitting a hammer on the side of a big tanker. No one hears it. I want a hammer that goes 'pong' to break the problem."

This manager recognized the importance of linking outsider-insiders to strategic imperatives where they can help to create the "pong" rather than leaving the random "pings" to happenstance. He wanted hundreds of organizational mechanics finding micro pulls (workplace challenges) where they would be hammering in unison to address the organization's macro challenges. In other words, he wanted outsider-insiders, from the executive suite to the assembly line, aligned around the key organizational objectives.

Creating a "pong" requires clearly articulated strategies and an organizational infrastructure (for example, communication channels, performance metrics, or rewards and recognition) that supports the implementation of new practices and processes. Alignment must occur at two decision points: (1) the selection of which challenges to work on, that is, picking the ones where gaps occurred between current assumptions and the root cause of problems that aligned with critical business challenges, and (2) the search for alternative or "outsider" approaches to address the root cause of those challenges that are aligned with overall business objectives. Outsider-insiders at the top, middle, and lower levels of the hierarchy must also be clear on their roles and responsibilities as outsider-insiders and supporters of fellow outsider-insiders.

Matching Outsider Views to Strategic Needs

Environmental changes set in motion a series of opportunities for pulls within individual firms. For example, the aftermath of the terrorist acts of September 11 and the decline in air travelers forced airline companies to reevaluate their pricing and operations. Similarly, in the wake of the demise of Enron, it became apparent that there was a conflict of interest in firms such as Arthur Andersen: the company was selling consulting advice while auditing its clients. This also led to a reexamination of the brokerage industry and the need to separate investment banking from corporate research. In all these cases, it was the competitive or political environment that created macro-level challenges that created opportunities to pull in new ideas. Successful senior executives are themselves outsider-insiders. They use their two hats to identify gaps between their organizations' current strategic direction and the demands of the competitive landscape.[1]

As shown in Figure 3.1, changes in organizational strategies usually create micro challenges at the working level. These become opportunities for outsider-insiders throughout the organization to identify gaps between current work practices and changes needed to address the new strategic objectives. Without alignment, various levels can easily go along their merry way in conflict with one another. Misalignment often occurs across functional units. A corporation embarks on a new outsourcing strategy, for instance, and the operations and procurement groups proceed to optimize their own objectives and end up working at cross-purposes. Here is an opportunity for outsider-insiders within each functional group to identify gaps and introduce new ways of working collaboratively to achieve the company's strategic objectives. That, in turn, may lead to revisions in functional strategies—the two-way arrow in Figure 3.1. As such, there is a dynamic interplay that occurs between the strategic and local levels as new ideas are introduced into an organization.

Figure 3.1. Aligning Strategic and Local-Level Change

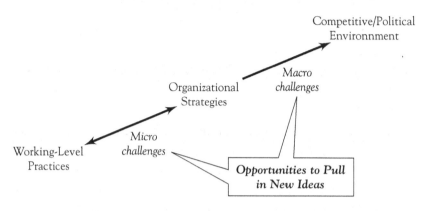

Consider the following example from American Diesel Corporation, where initial attempts to introduce new ideas were strongly resisted before a new manager stepped in to create alignment up and down the hierarchy.[2] By all accounts, the organization was achieving its strategic objectives to produce high-end diesel engines to a loyal customer base that was not considered particularly cost sensitive. A major global competitor, however, created a dramatic strategic challenge by entering the market with a lower-cost alternative engine. American Diesel's need to reduce costs drastically pulled in a new lean manufacturing strategy. But the implementation of that strategy ultimately had to occur at the workplace level.

As the new lean strategic initiative cascaded through the organization, it created a whole series of working-level challenges within American Diesel's manufacturing plants; in particular, it created micro pulls. But insiders who were not aware of the macro competitive challenge saw only a new initiative. Resultant changes to their local-level objectives and measurements felt like a push, as we saw in Chapter One with Worldwide Manufacturing Industries. This was especially true at American Diesel's Sedalia Engine Plant. The plant was recognized as a benchmark facility for its highly participative human resource strategy. As the managers within the plant responded to the new strategic initiative and began to rearrange the factory floor to reduce inventory, employees decried a loss of autonomy and participation in daily decision making. The problem was that the plant was locked into its historical work practices and assumptions around team member autonomy and empowerment. As inventory was reduced, employees could no longer choose to hold a team meeting or perform off-line staff-related duties whenever they pleased, a cornerstone of the design principles embedded into the participative management philosophy at the facility.

Outsider-insiders within the Sedalia operation could easily step back and see a gap between the existing human resource strategy and the new lean manufacturing initiative. The initial human resource practices were built on an assumption that inventory was good and provided time for employee autonomy by decoupling the various steps of the manufacturing process. Lean manufacturing, in contrast, views inventory as an evil that should be largely eliminated. Reducing inventory narrowed the opportunities for employee choice around work tasks, and team meetings or off-line duties had to be formally scheduled and staffed accordingly. For most employees, this felt like a push or corporate edict with no consideration of the negative ramifications at the workplace.

Clearly, American Diesel's executives needed mid- and working-level outsider-insiders within the Sedalia plant to create the "pong." They had to find individuals who knew how to wear two hats to help introduce lean practices. One such outsider-insider was a newly appointed plant manager at the Sedalia plant. He had previously been the human resource manager within the plant before becoming an operations manager at another facility. Brought back to the Sedalia plant because he clearly appreciated the cultural underpinnings of the operation, he also understood the new strategic imperatives.

The new plant manager quickly realized that the majority of the workforce was still working under the assumption that the plant was the benchmark for the industry; they didn't understand or believe that the corporation and the plant were facing a new competitive environment. As explained in Chapter Two, their cultural blinders were keeping them from seeing the challenge that required changes such as lean manufacturing practices. The plant manager decided to embark on a series of one-hour financial familiarization presentations for the entire workforce. He simply displayed the organization's financial results and tied them into the current market realities. He then had each of his staff members follow up with their groups to make sure everyone understood the message. Customers were brought into the facility to meet with employees and explain market realities. It was only after the message sank in that employees were open to implementing lean manufacturing tools, which they now recognized could help them attain new quality and productivity objectives.

The plant manager was also fortunate in that he knew many people in the plant from his earlier days as the human resource manager. He continued to nurture and build those relations through his personal style of spending a lot of time walking around the plant or joining employees for a beer after work. As a result, he quickly tapped into a network of fellow outsider-insiders throughout the plant: "There was a core group of folks who got it or just bought into it. They were my deputies that then went to others. They were the thought leaders within their teams. We sent many of them out on benchmarking trips and armed them with facts to go back to their teams."

True change began as employees came to realize that they really did need to adopt alternative work practices in order to respond to a macro-level pull and that the disciplined problem-solving methodology at the heart of lean manufacturing actually helped them to overcome problems they faced daily. Significantly, they also learned that collaborative teamwork could be as rewarding as individual autonomy.

Worldwide's Chicago operation (see Chapter One) and the Sedalia plant provide a clear distinction between top-down pushing and pulling change, and especially aligning pulls across the organization. Both corporations faced a macro challenge that created opportunities to pull in a new lean manufacturing strategy. Because Worldwide made the choice to go the push route, it made no effort to find and use outsider-insiders within the Chicago plant. If there were outsider-insiders internally, which is likely the case, no one heard them. There was no recognition of a need to look for gaps between current practices and assumptions and those needed to implement the new lean initiative. In contrast, the Sedalia plant was able to create a "pong" as a critical mass of outsider-insiders began questioning its own assumptions and began exploring alternative methods to overcome challenges. Today, the Sedalia plant stands as a benchmark within the company for the successful implementation of lean principles and has become the role model for other facilities within American Diesel.

Aligning the Organization

As we saw with the Sedalia case, alignment begins with creating a clear vision and helping insiders to see the need for change.[3] Once outsider-insiders understand the macro challenges and their organization's strategic objectives, they are in the position to identify daily challenges that provide an opportunity to pull in their outsider perspectives. But even when there is a recognized threat at the door, there is still a need for further alignment at a more tactical level. An executive outsider-insider who was assigned to help turn around a hemorrhaging manufacturing plant recalled:

> Everyone was running around like mice. The plant was on the chopping block but no one really knew it. I took my staff off-site for two Fridays. It was really good to have a week between the meetings for soak time—it wasn't planned that way; it was just when schedules would allow people to be away, but it worked out well. I told them that we were at a fork in the road and that we had options. At that point, we had five strategic objectives with five subbullets below each one. No one could focus on that many things. I gave them three things to focus on. . . . I concentrated on a one-voice

message to everyone with regular follow-up meetings. All of a sudden there was this huge surge of energy. In nine months we went from the most expensive to the least expensive plant in the division.

In this case, the executive's role was twofold: educate the plant concerning its competitive reality and his company's strategic goals and then align everyone around clearly defined tactical objectives. Fortunately, the challenges quickly became self-evident to all, and he was able to help working-level outsider-insiders focus their attention on identifying gaps between the current organizational assumptions and the root cause of the problems that were leading to the faculty's potential demise.

In many cases, critical organizational challenges are less apparent. Outsider-insiders often see gaps between assumptions and macro threats facing their organization before difficulties actually surface. They see where existing assumptions are likely to lead to problems. Obviously both outsider-insiders and their organizations would much rather preempt the problems than grapple with them as full-blown challenges. As described in Chapter Two, this means helping others to see what outsider-insiders observe. The task is to make the gaps evident. This means educating insiders on how to read external signals, similar to what the Sedalia plant manager did with his financial familiarization presentations. In operations terms, outsider-insiders must expose the parts of the icebergs that lie below the surface of the water.

When Lou Gerstner took over IBM, he saw how cultural assumptions were the root cause of the company's decline.[4] He went to great lengths to saturate himself into the IBM culture to become an outsider-insider. Having been a customer as well, he recognized the changing competitive landscape facing the computer industry. Customers no longer wanted to pick and choose different peripherals; they wanted totally integrated systems. Traditionally, however, each IBM product family acted as an independent business with its own marketing strategy and advertising agency. The problem was that insiders were totally oblivious to the fact that the company was sending out confusing and competing messages to their customers. To get the product managers to see the gap, Gerstner's marketing vice president posted each of the division's advertisements on a wall. The problem of conflicting messages quickly became evident to even the most strident insiders. In other words, one way to get insiders to see gaps is to make things visible through pictures.

Unfortunately, many insiders discount outsider perspectives that come from individuals who have spent their entire careers within the same organization. People from the outside, such as external experts, often have more credibility concerning impending macro-level competitive changes. In many ways, this was the dilemma Harry faced when he became vice president for operations at Niche Manufacturing. He had spent his entire career mostly in manufacturing and was always frustrated that the manufacturing function within Niche was viewed as a poor stepchild to research and product development. This was a deeply ingrained cultural assumption that stemmed from the belief system of the first CEO, a brilliant scientist who founded the company in the 1930s. As one manufacturing manager described it, "Manufacturing was viewed as 'those gorillas.' Our founder was rumored to have said, 'I design elegant products and those manufacturing folks screw them up.' We were viewed as second-class citizens."

When Harry joined the senior executive team, Niche was struggling in the marketplace because it was slower than its competitors in getting new products to market. Harry saw how the lower-class status of manufacturing was holding the company back from being a world-class competitor: manufacturing and engineering barely talked to one another. That this was a problem, however, was clearly an outsider perspective within the executive ranks. There were plenty of outsider-insiders who shared his vision within manufacturing, but any spark of desire to improve their image had long ago been beaten down by the engineering community, which viewed manufacturing as "an evil they had to deal with." Harry recognized that generating a "pong" across the entire corporation required creating outsider-insiders within the product development organization.

Harry's task was complicated by its organizational culture. The company's founder had created a strong paternalistic environment where every member of the "family" was given a voice, but he remained the dominant decision maker with his imprint embedded in just about every policy and procedure. As one outsider-insider said ruefully, "This is a company whose culture is still dominated by a man who's been dead for several years."

Harry knew he couldn't change the culture single-handedly. He needed a platform to enable a network of like-minded internal outsider-insiders to create the pong. He decided to tie his vision to a local university's newly formed industry consortium that was formed to improve manufacturing competitiveness. His strategy was to get as many managers and engineers as possible involved in consortium-related activities, such as seminars, presentations, and committees. One of his supporting outsider-insiders recalled,

> Niche's culture was one of involvement and participation, so you just couldn't dictate it. The idea was to get people involved and once they were involved, they would be committed. Our metric was the number of people involved in a year. . . . There was a conference where we sent seventy to a hundred people. We published a book of the proceedings. There was a huge company representation— maybe we over did it but it was the right thing for us to do. It played a major part in involving people.

Harry also invited some prestigious local academics to join an internal steering committee that would lead the effort. The academics provided the bait to lure representatives from key corporate functions, such as engineering, marketing, and finance, into joining the steering committee. The academics then introduced the idea of cross-functional collaboration and encouraged steering committee members to educate their organizations. During the following year, over twenty managers and engineers attended monthly seminars at the university. Within a couple of years, the strategy started to pay off. The most tangible result was a series of letters to the CEO concerning a proposed reorganization. As Harry recalled,

> We went through a process of getting input from the top sixty executives. Our CEO got twenty letters saying that the organization was fine except that manufacturing and product development should be combined in a separate organization and many of those letters used consortium-related terminology. Eight letters came from manufacturing and twelve from product development. We finally realized that we had to stop throwing it over the wall.

Harry's story is a clear example of a senior executive who had a clearly articulated vision, crafted an educational strategy that fit his organization's strategy, and then used the university consortium as the vehicle to communicate it. To the engineers and scientists, Harry was just one of the "gorillas" from manufacturing; he needed a messenger that would be respected and listened to by the technical community, and he got that with the engineering faculty from the local university. The result was an organization that visibly understood the macro challenges and aligned around the new vision. This set the stage for Harry's network of outsider-insiders to begin pulling in the new philosophy of integrating product development and manufacturing in solving product and process problems at the micro level.

Aligning Roles Within the Hierarchy

Outsider-insiders at the top of the hierarchy have a very different role from those at the working level. Obviously, in flat (or very small) organizations, these roles may merge, but by and large, stepping outside one's hierarchical role leads to mixed messages and stalled change efforts. For example, when senior executives attempt to apply outsider perspectives to solve a specific problem at the working level, they are typically viewed as micromanaging. And when frontline outsider-insiders attempt to make systemic changes or changes that do not align with their organization's strategic direction, they usually end up frustrated and shunned by their managers and peers.

As we saw with Harry, the top of the hierarchy, that is, the executive leadership team, is where the strategy must be set. Even in the most entrepreneurial organizations, someone must steer the ship and give guidance to the individuals creating the pings. This means that senior-level managers must identify and clearly articulate key strategic thrusts that will respond to macro challenges. Just publishing a strategic report is far from sufficient. Senior leaders must continually communicate what's important through both words and actions to create an environment that is receptive to outsider perspectives and empowers those who are able to appreciate the goals of the organization. This also means being a role model while developing and nurturing outsider-insiders throughout the organization that can respond to opportunities for micro pulls.

Once a critical mass of working-level outsider-insiders is attuned to the key strategies of a business, its combined efforts can lead to the "pong," provided the people are in a job where their two hats can be used, a task for the middle of the organizational hierarchy. Middle managers are best situated to match outsider perspectives to strategic needs and to link grassroots outsider-insiders to jobs where they can use their knowledge and skills to pull in new ideas or concepts. This is the role that the new plant manager at the Sedalia Engine Plant played, tapping into the outsider-insiders scattered throughout the plant. Often a skillful outsider-insider may reside within Division A of a company while a challenge that needs that individual's perspective is in Division B. Although there are job posting systems that can be used to help move people from one division to another, the most expedient way to match an outsider-insider to the challenge is through middle managers talking to other middle managers. As we will see in Chapter Seven, these middle managers end up creating an outsider-insider network, much like the "ring of openness" described in Chapter One, that provides the mechanism for helping working-level outsider-insiders get to the right place at the right time to use their two hats to help create the "pong." These middle managers also work to break down systemic barriers that are getting in the way of importing outsider perspectives and coach proactive outsider-insiders in how to leverage opportunities that will pull in change or new ideas.

Once the stage is set, outsider-insiders at the grassroots level can more effectively leverage opportunities to pull in change at a tactical (micro) level. They are the ones dealing with daily challenges that provide the opportunity for them to help others see where cultural assumptions are getting in the way of overcoming those challenges. But few working-level outsider-insiders have the influence or resources that executive outsider-insiders, such as Lou Gerstner, are privileged to possess. Instead, they must find daily, local levers to help educate their peers and managers. Like their senior-level outsider-insiders, they must become teachers helping others to see the value in questioning assumptions.

Does this sound like fantasyland? Is it really possible to expect large organizations to be completely aligned from top to bottom? Obviously, no organization is perfect, yet some come closer to the ideal than others, and the ideal is the target for organizations that want to be nimble and responsive to changing competitive environments. When this occurs, outsider-insiders feel valued and part of the family. That doesn't mean they lose their outsider perspectives; it just means that they have fewer roadblocks in their way. It's never simple, but as the following story illustrates, it is possible to align multiple levels of the hierarchy and then use informal networks to propagate outsider perspectives.

An Example of Aligning Macro and Micro Pulls

As a central component of a plan to improve competitiveness and become the world's leader in its industry (a macro challenge), Midwest Corporation's manufacturing organization embarked on an ambitious initiative to introduce a lean production system, which created opportunities for micro pulls within the plants. The existing culture at Midwest valued homegrown talent that had proven itself through long and grueling hours of dedication on the factory floor. Midwest's senior management recognized that to effectuate cultural change, it was crucial to bring young talent into manufacturing. But rather than bringing in new recruits to learn from the bottom up, Midwest chose to assign a group of young, high-potential engineers reporting directly to the vice president of manufacturing in a staff role. They were insiders who had already experienced the culture from the front lines and then had the opportunity to step outside for two years as full-time students in an advanced degree program that included internships at other companies. When they returned, now wearing two hats, they were eager to put their new perspectives to use in transforming their organization. But they encountered only resistance back on the shop floor.

They voiced their frustration to the vice president, who decided to have them act as internal consultants and help him introduce lean manufacturing concepts into Midwest. He assigned them a dual task: develop an educational program to educate the workforce about lean manufacturing and then facilitate the implementation of those principles. The group became known as the Lean University.

One of the first things group members did was to conduct interviews at all levels of the manufacturing organization. Although they personally believed that bottom-up change was the way to introduce the new lean concepts (in other words, find workplace or micro challenges to pull in the new ideas), the interviews reinforced what they had experienced earlier in their careers: Midwest's culture would question and defeat any grassroots efforts. As one of the Lean University members recalled, "The feedback was clear: 'Do not start at the bottom of the organization. . . . Don't get me all fired up and then not train the executives because they will just block whatever I try to do. They need to buy into it first.'"

As a result, they recommended that classes be cascaded from the top down. Although on the surface, this looks very similar to Worldwide Manufacturing Industries' lean training, the difference here was that the educational effort was a response to a macro challenge. As a result, the group developed course materials that each level of management, beginning with the executive vice president, taught to its subordinates. This approach was similar to one that Midwest had successfully used to roll out a new corporate mission. As the Lean University member described it,

> Basically, managers need to be more like coaches and teachers than the top-down autocrats that you tend to find in manufacturing. You cannot change the people and just bring in a whole new group of managers, so we decided to try to leverage the experience the organization had with rolling out the corporate mission. The mission was introduced through a cascade model starting at the top and going all the way through the company. So we decided that our model for education would also be a cascade.

Since the Lean University group's role was both to educate and begin the implementation of lean practices, it also initiated pilot projects within each plant to allow people on the shop floor to gain experience with the new operating principles. This, in essence, created opportunities to pull in lean concepts at a micro level. One of the outsider-insiders reported,

> We were really struggling with what the missing piece was that would allow the organization to change. We then started focusing on the link between education and change, between the "learn" and the "do" part. . . . We tried to focus on the shop floor and how to bring about change on the shop floor. We wanted to start small, to concentrate on changing a small area within the plant. This is where we came up with the idea of the pilot projects where people could apply the principles, translate the "learn" into "do."

The pilots provided hands-on practice to supplement the classroom teaching. But more important, they began to illustrate the value of the lean concepts. Despite initial skepticism and resentment, it took only one year for the lean production systems framework and the executive education program to be viewed as a success. Said one manager, "You know the power of it has gone beyond manufacturing. Earlier this week, I was at a top management meeting and people kept referring to Lean, including the CEO. It was mentioned more times than any other topic. Lean has become the focus for the entire company."

The final step was to disperse the Lean University group and rotate members out into the various plants to find further micro challenges where lean principles could be implemented. Every outsider-insider was strategically placed in a facility that was facing a significant and urgent challenge where they could use their expertise to find opportunities to pull in change. Furthermore, through their work with the Lean University, they had developed extensive networks of fellow outsider-insiders whom they could tap into to help propagate the "pong" throughout Midwest.

■ ■ ■

As each of the stories in this chapter has vividly illustrated, outsider-insiders must not only understand culture within their organizations to identify gaps, but they must also leverage those cultural norms to help others see the gaps. As one manager instructed, "You can only do it by talking the language of the culture. You have to take the ideas you learned and put them into a language where they can be understood. . . . You have to put it into a language that people can hear." This matching of alignment strategies to existing cultural norms is the topic we turn to in the following chapter.

Chapter Four

Working Within the Existing Culture to Pull Change

Change within organizations occurs within the context of the organization's existing culture. *Everything* occurs within that context: that is a fact of life. Outsider-insiders live within an existing culture, and it is current cultural assumptions that sustain the organization. There is a tendency, however, to look at existing cultures as barriers to change and assume that new ideas will take hold only if a cultural transformation happens. A cultural transformation may in fact be needed to institutionalize those ideas, but the existing culture is the reality, and it is only within this environment that outsiders-insiders can effect true change.[1] Moreover, outsider-insiders actually build off the existing ethos, leveraging the culture to ultimately change it. In sum, a culture can and should be leveraged, and it can evolve, but rarely, if ever, can "the culture" be fought.

Although it may seem counterintuitive, an organization's existing culture is one of the most effective levers for initiating cultural change. It's called "working the system." Consider Rustbelt Corporation, a traditional, old-line manufacturing bureaucracy with entrenched functional silos and an autocratic, top-down hierarchical power base that celebrates internal experience over expertise. One of Rustbelt's difficulties in bringing in new people was that recruits were traditionally put through a lengthy socialization period to test whether they were tough enough to survive. One of the managers recalled his "hazing" period:

> The first five years at Rustbelt were the most abusive of my career. It was pay your dues and showtime. Showtime is showing that you

are committed to working twenty hours/day to show your value. . . .
For the first five years, I was not expected to have any creativity or
any good ideas. You are just expected to perform and do it the same.
I remember being the "college boy" and having to live with the
pompous old managers who said, "I've done it this way for twenty-
five years." . . . The people would relish making new people with
prestigious credentials hurt even more. It was a red flag. They licked
their lips to make life terrible for them. It was just macho bullshit.

When the company launched a major restructuring effort to
integrate engineering and manufacturing, these two organizational
"chimneys" needed to work together to respond to a dramatic competitive need. As was the case at Niche Manufacturing, decades
of finger-pointing at Rustbelt had evolved into vicious distrust
between the functions. This disdain stemmed from not understanding what each other did and not having any desire or opportunity to move between the silos. As a result, most of Rustbelt's
managers lacked the needed skills to make the transition toward
integration. Moreover, the workforce was mostly born and bred in
the local metropolitan area; they were all insiders who had not
been exposed to outsider perspectives. But unlike Niche, there
were a few outsider-insiders, especially at the working level. "We
needed to change our paradigm," one noted. "We needed to develop
links with people who would provide a different perspective, who
were more open."

Rather than just going out and hiring a batch of handpicked
external managers to help drive the change, Rustbelt's executive-
level outsider-insiders decided to bring in young "future leaders" and
accelerate their ascent through the ranks. The intent was to help
these recruits quickly develop into outsider-insiders (people wearing
two hats) and then prepare them so that they could rapidly get to an
influential position to lead further cultural change within four or five
years rather than the traditional twenty years that the culture
expected. The hope was that as they moved through the organization, they would help to begin pulling in change from the bottom
up. But first they needed to quickly ascend to leadership roles in the

middle management ranks where they could help to develop the next wave of working-level outsider-insiders. Given the company's macho culture, these new developing outsider-insiders would be "eaten alive" if they didn't have the protection of senior-level outsider-insider champions.

As the outsider-insider veterans recognized, a direct assault on the culture would create chaos and potential revolt. The executives knew that they alone could not drive the change from the top. Pushing change, even in a top-down, autocratic culture, creates only lipservice if there are no supporting outsider-insiders at the middle and lower levels of the organization looking for opportunities to pull in the new desired behaviors. The "veterans" decided to leverage that top-down dominated style to create an infrastructure to recruit, nurture, and protect new talent. Their aim was to develop working-level outsider-insiders who could use their two-hat abilities to identify daily challenges that engineering and manufacturing could quickly resolve by working together.

Rustbelt began by creating a structured leadership development program that included executive-level sponsorship and rotational assignments whereby the recruits were strategically placed in cross-functional assignments. The program was championed and closely monitored by the senior executive outsider-insiders; after all, this was a culture that responded to senior-level edicts, and the executives used this norm to place these new employees in positions where they could learn the culture (become insiders) while demonstrating the value of outsider perspectives. The developing outsider-insiders were given an expressed goal of identifying challenges that cut across the functional silos. Although they lacked the clout as newcomers and were in assignments for only nine to twelve months (not long enough to make large-scale changes), they were asked to identify issues for senior management to begin working the system from above. So even in their short-term assignments, they were expected to initiate the pulling change cycle by identifying gaps between current assumptions and the root cause of daily problems they encountered.

On the surface, Rustbelt's leadership development program looked like many other corporations' fast-track career paths, but the hidden beauty of the program was that it was designed for and being used to help pull in new concepts in response to a macro-level challenge. As one of the executives described,

> We want to harvest a benefit from these people. . . . This is not a training program. It is a learn as you go program. The clock does not drive development; it is performance that drives development. . . . We expect them to deliver three things on each assignment: they need to produce on the assignment, they are expected to do a cross-organization project, and they are to identify a broader problem and leave it for others, such as future new entrants or upper management, to pick up.

Once each quarter, the executives met with the new recruits to share their strategic vision and help build mentoring relationships. In addition to learning where the problem spots were, the executives helped steer their developing outsider-insiders in a direction that would help facilitate their desired major restructuring effort, that is, align macro and micro pulls. Their performance on the job served two purposes: show a payback for the leadership program and build individual credibility within the organization. Hence, the key to their survival was to learn about the existing culture quickly. One of the executives explained the process: "If you really want to, you can really make a difference. But you have to understand the system. Then you have a chance to do what you really want. If you really want to change something and don't get stuck in the muck, you can. You just have to figure out how to do it within the system."

The executives at Rustbelt recognized the power of culture. They wanted an organization where working-level outsider-insiders could use their two hats to pull in ideas to improve the operation without constant surveillance by senior leadership. But they knew they lived in a top-down-dominated organization, and any change had to begin within that environment. Rather than making a frontal assault on the existing culture, they figured out a clever way to use the culture to accelerate the development of a new cadre of leaders who would work from the bottom of the hierarchy and build a critical mass of new perspectives to accelerate what amounted to cultural change. There is no question that they pushed these developing outsider-insiders into the organization, a necessary first step in a hierarchical risk-averse culture. They took the risk to jump-start the process with a strong initiative to get outsider-insiders into a position where they could find opportunities to begin pulling in improvement ideas throughout the company. Once a critical mass of outsider-insiders was thereby developed, they could help respond to future macro and micro pulls. They were en route to true change.

Cultures like that at Rustbelt can be quite frustrating, but they do change, even toward true change, and they can be "worked." Such companies' mere survival is testimony to the fact that they have responded to economic or environmental challenges. If they hadn't, they would have gone out of business. In other words, previous outsider-insiders were astute enough to find opportunities to leverage those strongly entrenched organizational cultures. And as Rustbelt's executives demonstrated, the process of pulling in change into an established culture works only when change advocates fully understand the existing cultural norms and use that culture to transform it. A senior manager at another traditional hierarchical company echoed a similar sentiment: "Infusion doesn't work; you can't just take something and put it in place without the culture. You have to understand the value of it. Do you have any appreciation of what it takes to change something in this company? You have to get leverage. You have to use collateral issues in a major organization."

Sometimes the learning and credibility-building process for newly minted outsider-insiders can be painstakingly slow, because many cultures are not as self-evident as Rustbelt's. Even companies with clearly articulated, espoused values and processes have cultural nuances that only reflective insiders can see. Furthermore, companies typically have a complex mix of subcultures, many of them legacy cultures within divisions or locations resulting from previous mergers and acquisitions. The trick is to understand how change has previously been accomplished, that is, deciphering avenues to leverage the organization's openness to new ideas and then working within that culture rather than fighting it.

Matching Pulling Change Strategies to the Existing Culture

Each organization is, of course, unique and has its own set of norms and assumptions. How outsider-insiders in a hierarchical top-down organization go about helping others see gaps between their current assumptions and the challenges they are facing is very different from how outsider-insiders within an entrepreneurial, fast-paced environment might approach the same task. Risk-averse organizations like Rustbelt that tend to value experience over scientific reasoning rely heavily on the hierarchy for communications and decision making and require senior-level or influential advocates for new or outsider perspectives. That means that young, working-level outsider-insiders must tap into the power structure and find veteran outsider-insiders to help insiders see how their cultural assumptions are getting in the way of solving the challenges they face. By comparison, outsider-insiders living within entrepreneurial environments that tend to be more data driven and horizontally networked must rely more on their lateral relationships and use scientific reasoning to convince others that there are gaps in their thinking. Obviously, these two extreme profiles can easily lead to superficial stereotyping. Each organization must be analyzed on its own since every culture has its own unique web of assumptions. Nevertheless, outsider-insiders must be cognizant of their environment and match their approach to pulling change to the existing norms.

Two quick snapshots highlight the importance of working within a culture when approaching opportunities to pull in new ideas. Sue works in an entrepreneurial, technocratic organization. As an engineer, she has a degree of credibility based on her credentials, but she also recognizes critical characteristics of her organization's culture and how to capitalize on them. Her company was one of the more mature high-technology firms in its industry, founded more than seventy years ago as one of the country's early electronics companies. Gaining advocacy played a major part in building support for new ideas. This aspect of the culture was a reflection of its paternalistic roots: most families have hierarchies, and parents still want to approve each new generation's ideas. Using data to build her case, Sue convinced her manager of the value of a new approach to analyzing product defects. Her manager then became her advocate and shared the idea with his network to build support for implementation. As she explained,

> The culture is really open to change. . . . If you have good ideas, you just have to sell them. You have to have good presentation skills and have data to show. It is really a data-driven culture. Managers are very rational. . . . It was helpful to work closely with my mentor. He was in a position of influence. It was just getting the facts, showing the benefits, starting small, and showing the worth. There were definitely key supporters that allowed it to proliferate out.

Now let's look at a similar situation in a more risk-averse environment. Bill works at a more traditional, hierarchical company that is generally quite resistant to new concepts or ways of doing things. In many respects, it was quite similar to Rustbelt, but it also overtly values technical expertise. Bill had worked in engineering for fifteen years before transferring to manufacturing and was therefore an outsider-insider within his company's manufacturing function. As he approached the task of introducing his outsider perspectives, he used his network of friends and prior work associates to tap into and work the hierarchical power structure to cross functional silos. As he described,

> Since I came up through the engineering function and am now in manufacturing, I'm viewed as "an insider outside of my chain." I only survive because my mentor, one of the VPs, looks over me. We meet monthly. . . . I was in manufacturing for three months, and I was pitching an idea to corporate that folks in manufacturing had spent four years on but needed numerical control programming and software support to make it happen. So I went and got a buddy I knew from engineering. Typically someone in computer services would never work with or on a problem with someone in manufacturing. Anyway, I went to my mentor and told him what we had found, and he went to the VP in charge of the operation. He also told me to pitch it to a third key manager who had influence with the operations VP. The manager then talked to the operations VP, to whom my mentor had already talked. Then we went to corporate to sell the idea.

Both Sue and Bill understood the importance of working within their existing organizational culture to pull in alternative mental models to solve existing challenges. Imagine what would have happened if they switched companies but failed to change their strategies in selling their ideas! Sue's approach would have never seen the light of day at Bill's company, or it would have taken eons for her idea to make it up the hierarchy to be sanctioned. Similarly, Bill's efforts to work the hierarchy would have been unnecessary in Sue's organization and might have bred resentment in the middle management ranks.

In both cases, their personalities and approaches to introducing new ideas fit their respective organizations. They knew their respective organization's cultures and understood how to work within them. But Sue and Bill were also fortunate to have support systems that recognized the power of their outsider-insider perspectives (see Chapters Five through Seven). Their managers and mentors helped them identify opportunities to pull in new ideas aligned to their respective organization's key strategies that were in place to address macro challenges. Hence, matching strategies for pulling change to the existing culture is the second half of outsider-insider success. In other words, pulling change requires two complementary components: alignment and matching.

Understanding the Context for Pulling Change

The message here is quite simple: before you can work successfully within an existing culture to find opportunities to pull in new ideas, you must first understand the organization's norms and assumptions. This may appear self-evident, but my research says *not so*. I found that many aspiring "change agents" are unable to decipher, or are oblivious to, key cultural enablers to implementing new ideas. Time and again, I found managers who ignored the need to tailor their approach to introducing new ideas to the existing context. Many just assumed that others would naturally see their logic, and if they didn't, those people were stupid or just resistant. Others simply assumed that the culture was an inmovable object that would inevitably block the adoption of new ideas. The astute ones, however, recognized the key components of their culture and leveraged them in order to get others to consider alternative approaches.

Overall, organizational cultures are intricate webs of overlapping and reinforcing assumptions about how the world works. Many of those assumptions are what drive an organization to be successful. Others, however, inhibit it from being even better than it is. It's the latter that outsider-insiders want to change, but dislodging a single assumption is like playing pick-up sticks: pulling out one stick can bring the rest of the pile crashing down on the player. The secret is to find those assumptions that are blocking the achievement of key challenges and then look for "structural beams" that can be leveraged to maintain support while removing the blockers. Figure 4.1 highlights three key structural beams that can provide leverage for outsider-insiders: (1) the criteria organizations use to evaluate ideas, that is, the basis for legitimacy; (2) to whom organizational members listen, that is, the basis for relationships; and (3) whether outsider perspectives need influential champions, that is, the basis for support. As we will see, these three structural beams tend to reinforce one another to create a platform for introducing new ideas.

Each "beam" represents a continuum of assumptions between two extreme, stereotypical cultures. Few organizational cultures reside totally at either end of the continuum. Using the bookends for contrast, however, provides a glimpse of the various artifacts that outsider-insiders need to decipher. We'll start by looking at the characteristics of firms at each end of the three continua. But first, one caveat: cultural levers can change over time. Many start-up companies are characterized by the attributes on the left-hand side of Figure 4.1. But as they grow, they often tend to gravitate to the right.[2]

Basis for Legitimacy

We all would like to believe that logic rules when it comes to decision making and the acceptance of new ideas, but that is not always the case, especially since the objectivity of data or the best approach to addressing a problem is in the eye of the beholder. Hence, outsider-insiders must understand the basis for credibility of ideas

Figure 4.1. Context for Pulling Change

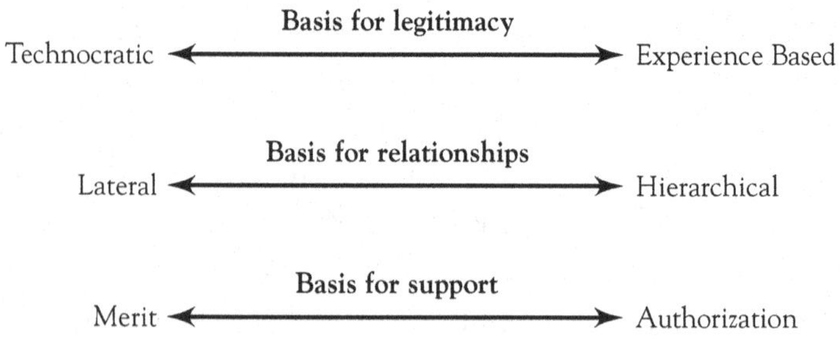

Basis for legitimacy

Technocratic ← → Experience Based

Basis for relationships

Lateral ← → Hierarchical

Basis for support

Merit ← → Authorization

within a given culture in order to know how to frame their ideas so they will be accepted. How the case for change is developed, to whom it is presented, and how the story is told are often as important as, if not more important than, the story itself.

Technocratic

Firms that are founded by technologists typically place a high value on engineering or analytical thinking. To be heard, one must first build credibility through a proven track record of technical competence. Having an engineering or science degree is a prerequisite for building credibility, but to gain insider status one must also demonstrate technical competence. Outsider-insiders who identify a need to bridge silos in technocratic cultures must first build credibility as a discipline specialist before trying to sell cross-functional ideas. As one such outsider-insider reflected, disciplinary experts are valued more than generalists: "You need to be an expert before you can talk in general. So you need to be a specialist in an area with general applications. . . . Technical ability is a critical factor."

The implication for less technical outsider-insiders is that they must work with the "deep geeks" to build credibility for their outsider perspectives. Fortunately, data are king in most technocratic cultures, a prerequisite in the packaging of any new ideas. "People are very data driven," affirmed one manager, basing his acknowledgment of the importance of "scientific reasoning." "They won't believe what you say or accept your ideas," he continued, "unless you have concrete data to support what you're saying."

This is good news for outsider-insiders since data can usually talk louder than functional loyalties, age, seniority, or internal politics. Lou Gerstner, for instance, was able to leverage the importance of clear logic in the technocratic culture at IBM. Each product line was concerned about its own turf. But when leaders of the various product divisions were faced with definitive evidence that separate advertising campaigns were sending conflicting messages, they quickly acquiesced to a more centralized message. The overriding value of data within the culture transcended functional squabbling.

The strong focus on data in technocratic firms, however, can sometimes hinder the introduction of such concepts as organizational learning, since these are less easily quantifiable. Technologists consider themselves to be logical people who look at solutions from a purely scientific perspective. They have little patience for team building or other so-called softer activities that take them away from rational, analytical problem solving, so ideas that are more difficult to quantify must be bundled with more technical changes. One manager explained the approach: "The environment here in the technical ranks is very analytical. Most managers come from a technical foundation, and the way they think about problems is pretty pragmatic. They organize their problems for analytical thinking—they use data and strong logic and rational thinking. We bundle changes in organizational practices with emerging process technologies, so timing is critical."

This notion of bundling is a prime example of how culture can be leveraged. By timing the introduction of new organizational ideas with the launch of a new generation of a product or a major technical change in the operation, outsider-insiders can show how new organizational concepts will help to facilitate the introduction of new technology. Furthermore, any associated training needed for the new organizational concepts can be bundled with the technical instruction for the new technology. In this way, the scientists and engineers do not feel they are "wasting their time" on non-technical issues.

Experience Based

At the other end of the spectrum are experience-based cultures that tend to use seniority, age, and company longevity as the basis for valuing an employee's worth and knowledge. This comment captures it all: "Terry was perceived as, 'What could you possibly know if you haven't been here for ten years?'"

Rustbelt was a prime example of an experience-based culture. New recruits had to spend five years paying their dues to build credibility before anyone would even consider listening to their analysis of a situation. And that was just the initial indoctrination period. It took *another* fifteen years to get to a position before they could begin influencing the implementation of new concepts. Rustbelt is not alone. Many experience-based companies still look at employees as lifers, even in an economy where lifetime employment has long been a thing of the past.

Furthermore, socialization processes emphasize the need to conform to insider ways of doing things in experience-based organizations. Maintaining an ability to wear two hats after a twenty-year socialization process is difficult, to say the least. Those outsider-insiders who are able to maintain outsider perspectives, such as Rustbelt's executives, learned to cleverly leverage their veteran status to build credibility for alternative ways of doing things. But "youngsters," even if they are adults, are expected to listen to their elders rather than voice their opinion. As a result, outsider-insiders new to an experience-based company have an uphill battle and must find organizational veterans who are sympathetic to their views and work with them to present new ideas. In contrast, outsider-insiders in technocratic organizations, provided they have a technical background no matter what their age, just need to build their case based on logic and data and then find a sympathetic audience.

Although these cultural attributes tend to span the organization, functions can exhibit individual cultural characteristics of their own, as was the case at Niche Manufacturing. The engineering community was more technocratic and responded to local academics who were well-respected experts in their fields. Manufacturing was more experience based, which fueled a perceived status differential: scientists versus "gorillas." Harry fully recognized this distinction and used the academic experts to tell the story in engineering while he used his own experience and credibility within manufacturing to build a case for outsider perspectives.

Basis for Relationships

In addition to knowing how to tell the story, outsider-insiders also need to learn whom they need to tell the story to. Those who have been successful in introducing new ideas have discovered that who you know or interact with is often as important as how good your ideas may be. Networks are the way that information is exchanged in most organizations. Granted, there are formal communication channels, but when it gets down to tapping into influential contacts, networks are much more effective and expedient. As one manager noted, "I tell new recruits that the success factor for people is to find your network. I've had varied jobs. . . . I've gotten to know a lot of people that way, so through a couple of phone calls, I finally find the right people. You can't go to the organization chart or a centralized database; you have to find the keepers of the connections."

Networks are basically "who talks to whom" and based on assumptions around what are considered important relationships to develop. These relationships determine the influence that various individuals have and how that power is developed—the second structural beam that provides leverage for introducing new ideas. As we saw, both Bill and Sue tapped into internal networks to help sell their perspectives, but those networks were quite different: Sue used her mentor's peer or lateral network for building support for her outsider ideas, and Bill worked a more hierarchical set of contacts.

Lateral

Despite formal hierarchies and functional silos, many organizations foster environments in which lateral relationships are the key to decision making, getting things done, and knowledge exchange. Power and influence arise through an ability to build horizontal relationships rather than hierarchical position. In many entrepreneurial companies, hierarchies exist only for coordination purposes, and every level of the organization is empowered to "make the right decision." That doesn't mean the "network" goes away, however. As one manager noted of his entrepreneurial firm, "The company is not hierarchical. You can make things happen even if you are two levels below. You just have to figure out who are the right people to talk to."

In organizations built on lateral relationships, horizontal networks are the way to stay attuned to what's happening. Furthermore, developing and nurturing these networks is key to getting anything accomplished. As another manager noted, "It is really just figuring out whom you need to get information from and how to get it."

Although lateral relationships are usually associated with more entrepreneurial organizations, the lateral networks often become the default mechanism for making things happen in highly matrixed companies. In such organizations, it is clear that lateral connections are critical to one's success. "Touching bases" is a fundamental part of the implementation of any new idea, as a senior manager pointed out: "This company is an extremely matrixed company, so a network of personal relationships is really important. A lot of things don't happen through the hierarchy. It requires much more consensus building. The requirement [is] to make the sale on multiple fronts." Furthermore, these horizontal relationships serve to build a critical mass of support for outsider perspectives, as will be discussed in Chapter Seven.

Hierarchical

At the other end of the continuum are more traditional organizations where peer communications across functions must go up the ladder in one silo to an executive decision maker before coming back down to a counterpart in another one—what is often referred to as moving up and down an "inverted U" on the organization chart. As one outsider-insider noted, this attitude slows problem solving and integration across functional lines: "Hierarchy is very evident in this company. . . . Production and Engineering are used to deferring up the organizational ladder regarding problems. Problems tend to rise to a level where someone with the required power level in the hierarchy can pressure the other functional group into action."

Introducing outsider perspectives in hierarchical organizations means touching bases vertically. Skipping levels is unheard of. Even in making presentations, each rung of the hierarchy has to buy off on the content and be comfortable with the message before those above can be exposed to the message. This is the environment that the Lean University group found at Midwest. As we saw, they created a top-down cascading training program to make sure that each level of the hierarchy knew that its bosses had already gone through the training.

Power in top-down organizations is determined by hierarchical rank. In many respects, these cultures are much easier, albeit more frustrating, to navigate since where the power lies is fairly transparent: it is the person who has the largest corner office. These organizations generally have a culture dominated by top-down decision making, where employees defer to senior management. For Rustbelt, this transparency made it easier for senior leaders to place developing outsider-insiders throughout the organization. The executives also created a formal hierarchical network with their quarterly meetings. On the one hand, this reinforced the hierarchical nature of relationships at Rustbelt; on the other hand, it leveraged that same cultural trait.

Although networks, whether they are lateral or hierarchical, are essential, they are not sufficient. Networks can simply be reference points unless the nodes are also locations of outsider-insiders who share a similar vision. As we will see in Chapter Seven, these networks must provide a conduit for identifying opportunities to pull in change. They should be the mechanism to help outsider-insiders get to the right place at the right time to introduce new ideas.

Basis for Support

The third structural beam for leveraging change is the basis on which new ideas gain support—that is, who backs up the story. Many organizations are so large and complex that new ideas rarely see the light of day unless there is a champion supporting and protecting the messengers or, better yet, acting as an advocate and greasing the way for outsider-insiders. Hence, outsider-insiders need to find influential champions to help them in their efforts to pull in new mental models that run counter to the existing culture. Performance-based cultures or meritocracies, by comparison, rarely require formal advocates. Ideas rise and fall on their own merits. The criteria for evaluating or supporting outsider perspectives are whether they produce desired results and are aligned to macro challenges; both are required.

Merit

Meritocracies are rooted in a belief that performance can be measured quantitatively and fairly. As long as desired results follow, one can generally just go and try out new ideas. One entrepreneurial outsider-insider captured his organization's culture precisely: "You are allowed to do whatever you want as long as you produce results."

Not surprisingly, meritocracies are often an outgrowth of data-driven, technocratic cultures. These companies also tend to be more egalitarian, with little preferential treatment afforded hierarchical position. In fact, the need for formal mentors to develop outsider-insiders, such as we saw at Rustbelt, would be viewed as a crutch in a meritocracy, a sign of weakness. *Can't these people stand on their own two feet?* it might be asked. Meritocracies demand assertiveness from their outsider-insiders. No one will be herding or guiding them into opportunities to effectuate change; they must do it on their own. A potential downside to this laudable individualism, however, is that risk taking can be extremely costly if the results are not immediately obvious. As one manager warned, "You have to take the risk and take charge. Risk taking is a part of ownership. If you are wrong, you will get whacked hard. So you better hope you are not wrong most of the time. Some people avoid that sort of thing."

Furthermore, when a proposed change is large enough or systemic in nature, it helps to have a support base. As one manager put it: "You can take the risks here, but if you make any big changes, you cannot do it yourself." Support is built by touching bases with one's lateral relationships, as noted above, rather than looking upward for hierarchical support, as is necessary at the other end of the basis for support continuum. In other words, individuals do not feel it necessary to involve their managers if they can work an issue at their own level, even if it means working across functional chimneys.

Authorization

In authorization cultures, advocates for new ideas or alternative approaches to doing things must be found. Merit or data alone are not sufficient; new ideas or concepts need a stamp of approval from someone who "counts." In fact, many people are willing to try new ideas only if influential champions have sanctioned them, meaning both the people and the ideas. This, in essence, is protection for going out on the limb and trying something unconventional. In authorization cultures, however, regardless of whether the desire for having protection is individual, the demand for it is organizational. Ideas *must* have sanction, not only support. The authorization does not necessarily need to be top down, but it does need to come from influential people. This is not a misspelling of "authoritarian": the approval must come from an individual whose expertise, not dictatorial power, is unquestionable. Thus, in experience-based firms, authorization may come from "gray hairs"—people with long-standing tenure. But in hierarchical environments, it helps to have a directive come directly from other kinds of seniors, that is, from the top, regardless of longevity. Thus, the need for authorization was a primary reason the Lean University team at Midwest decided to have next-level-up managers and supervisors serve as co-trainers in the educational design: having bosses deliver the training reinforced the message that they believed in and supported the new lean concepts.

Developing outsider-insiders in authorization environments needs formal support and protection, the role that the senior executives played at Rustbelt. The corporate immune system will "eat them up" if they try to do it on their own as their meritocratic brethren do. One hesitant outsider-insider at another hierarchical company lamented, "I wouldn't take a stand unless I had strong backing from management. You definitely can't go out on a limb here." But as we will see in Chapter Seven, advocacy must be earned to have legs. It is not something that comes without strings: performance must follow or advocacy quickly vanishes.

Organizational Openness to Change

While all organizations exhibit resistance to new ideas or change in one form or another, some tend to be more receptive than others. The twelve companies that constituted the research on culture and change discussed in this chapter revealed an additional continuum of cultural assumptions concerning openness to change. Although many of the companies are quite diversified, with numerous local cultures within their various divisions, businesses, or sites, there was always a single set of underlying assumptions about how one goes about making change. In other words, each company had its own distinct organizational reaction to change.

As shown in Figure 4.2, the vast majority of the companies fell into a category we labeled risk averse because new ideas were typically shunned, at least initially. This doesn't mean that new ideas were not implemented; many were. Yet the underlying assumptions that emerged from people in these organizations suggested that one should always expect significant resistance to any new ideas. This was especially true in organizations like Rustbelt, where there are multiple layers of entrenched managers between the fresh voices and the champions who proclaim they want change. Nevertheless, the senior executives at Rustbelt *did* understand key cultural assumptions and were in a position to work with those assumptions to change them, as we have seen.

Not all companies, of course, immediately assume that new ideas are problematic. In entrepreneurial organizations, innovation

Figure 4.2. Cultural Openness to Change

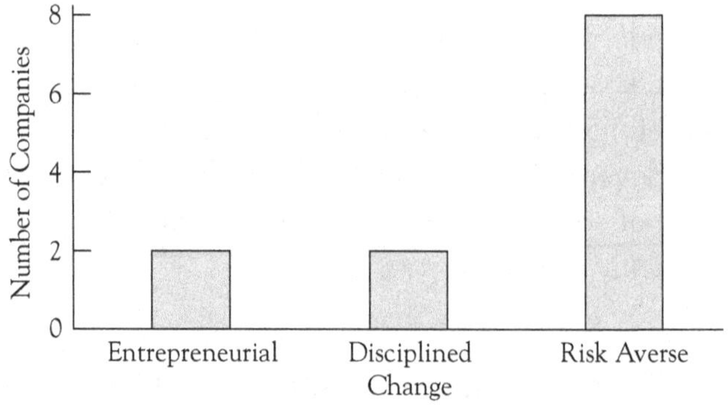

is an expected norm. But outsider perspectives are still eschewed, especially if they require coordination across individuals. A common phrase used by people who have managed entrepreneurial organizations is that it feels like "herding cats" to implement any systemic change. As a result, some organizations have developed processes to channel entrepreneurial efforts. These firms encourage change but only when it is done in a disciplined manner. In other words, change within these firms is an expected part of life, but there are strict norms about how new ideas should be introduced. Below we explore the good, the bad, and the ugly of each orientation to change.

Risk Averse

It is a truism that most large corporations are risk averse when it comes to change, and our group of twelve companies is no exception. Their size and bureaucratic policies and procedures lead their employees to be conservative and particularly resistant to change. One manager recalled a clear message to walk the party line from the day he joined the company: "It was a culture of don't make waves. When I first came into the company, I can remember being told, 'We don't need to change that, there is no reason to change even if there really was a reason, or we've done it this way forever, why do we need to change?'"

Even if a risk-averse organization experiences financial trouble, many employees tend to believe that their company is just "too big to fall," even when abundant evidence elsewhere is to the contrary. One frustrated outsider-insider lamented, "The attitude of most employees is that the company has deep pockets and I'll retire before it falls." The tumbling of giant corporations, such as Arthur Andersen and Enron, has helped to temper these attitudes, but organizational complacency still exists. Over the years, people have become personally risk averse due to fears that the organization will sacrifice advocates of change. We heard over and over again how this conservativism led to hedging and indecisive decision making, even in companies that espoused risk taking, as one outsider-insider observed: "You are constantly being told that you are to be a risk taker but there are penalties to be paid if you take risks and fail. As a result, people commonly look like they are risk takers, but they hedge their bets."

But what is often perceived as a cautious approach to change has roots in a belief that decision making must be inherently conservative because changing product or process technology must be inherently costly. This attitude is especially true in highly intensive, integrated process industries where reams of data are needed to back up any proposed change. Although rigorous analysis and documentation are often quite legitimate when, for example, moving a process line can cost up to $10 million, the paperwork looks overly bureaucratic to impatient proponents of change. In other words, there is a confusion between the paper consumed in form filling and the dollars required for technology change.

Risk-averse organizations do not change overnight. But they do embark on the effort, as evidenced by several companies in our study that were navigating tumultuous waters, moving leftward on the openness-to-change dimension. Change often comes through small wins that slowly multiply. Outsider-insiders must therefore be "practical radicals" who recognize that persistent patience is the road to successfully finding opportunities for pulling in change.[3] It also means finding legitimacy and support for what may be viewed as radical thinking. Risk aversion is, ultimately, another cultural lever that can be itself pulled.

Entrepreneurial

At the other extreme are entrepreneurial organizations that tend to consist of strong individualists, often referred to as "cowboys," who love coming up with new ideas. Both of our entrepreneurial organizations were well-established multinational companies, not start-ups as one might think. They had proud ingrained cultures that had survived and flourished over many years—one for over thirty years, the other for more than seven decades. Although both had traditional hierarchies, employees had enormous autonomy to "invent." One outsider-insider explained, "If you have an idea and you can find support to get money and cover, then you can run with it. It is a very entrepreneurial culture. I like to think of it as an organic model. . . . You plant five or ten or fifty seeds, and they will grow into little businesses and self-organize. That is really the model for the culture."

On the surface, an entrepreneurial culture is nirvana for implementing new ideas, but any attempt at changing the culture, especially to institute more disciplined problem solving or common work processes, is typically viewed as a reduction of individual or group autonomy. Trying to lead organized change goes against the grain of the culture (recall the "herding cats" description above). As one manager proudly noted, "If you told people to go down the hall and go right, half will go right and half will go left. Then we will debate it."

In organizations composed of "cohabitating entrepreneurs" who are rewarded as individuals for new ideas, there is often a general reluctance to reuse other people's concepts. This can be quite frustrating for outsider-insiders who want to import external ideas. As one manager explained, knowledge reuse is often shunned: "You don't get a lot of points for adapting someone else's information; therefore there's a NIH (Not Invented Here) syndrome. The mentality is, 'How can you be a leader if you are adapting someone else's information?'"

Hence, entrepreneurial environments are not as easy for introducing new ideas as one might expect. The good news is that the high value placed on invention and individual achievement makes it relatively straightforward to find opportunities to pull in change into an isolated area, but pulling that change through the organization can be extremely challenging.

Disciplined Change

In between the two extreme ends of the openness-to-change dimension are organizations that temper entrepreneurial aggressiveness with strong cultural norms around how to initiate change. Two of the companies in our study fit this profile. Both value "bounded risk taking"—provided all change occurs through a process that adheres to established organizational norms. These processes are instilled into the workforce from day one. They are taught during employee orientations, role-modeled by every level of the organization from top to bottom, and incorporated into performance evaluations. It is a conscious effort not left to happenstance. The end result is that the process one uses to attain results is as important as the results themselves. "Good results that create disharmony are not welcome," one manager explained. "It is viewed as rocking the boat and not having the proper balance between process and outcomes."

The trick for individuals who aim to introduce new ideas is to learn the "harmony" logic and then put their entrepreneurial spirit to work in a disciplined manner that fits within their organization's cultural norms. It takes a disciplined outsider-insider to understand the system and not be frustrated by it. One successful outsider-insider described the rules of the game for introducing new ideas in his operation: "Change has to happen in a controlled process. In order to figure out a good way to fix something, you have to have data. To implement a change, you have to document the problem, do the statistical analysis to prove that it is a valid improvement and that it does not make anything else worse. And if you can do all that, you can make change."

For outsider-insiders who accept, and are comfortable with, working within those boundaries, finding opportunities to pull outsider perspectives into and throughout the organization can be fairly uncomplicated. People who are impatient or truly unconventional thinkers, however, can become quite discouraged. This was the case with one proactive outsider-insider who got a little too entrepreneurial and had his wings clipped in the process, as one of his peers explained: "Clarence was very frustrated by his inability to make changes. Managers weren't willing to let him experiment."

The key to having a disciplined change culture is having people who are comfortable with the rules of the game but never complacent with the status quo, a fine balance between control and autonomy. One outsider-insider noted, "Our structured processes are one way that we can still allow change while keeping control and accelerating the rate of improvement. I think it is perceived as a stopgap, but it is a filter."

In many respects, disciplined change offers the best of both worlds. But it is an environment that requires continual nurturing and is not necessarily appropriate for every situation. Furthermore, many people do not fit the strict norms set by companies that follow a pattern of disciplined change. Outsider-insiders, by definition, must be comfortable working within their organization's cultural expectations, part of the insider equation. But they need the support of their organization to wear their outsider hat, which is what we turn to in the remainder of this book.

Building an Organizational Capability for True Change

Now that we have explored the framework for pulling change and the need to align pulls with strategic objectives and match them to the existing culture, it is time to turn to the third key ingredient for true change. As shown in Figure 4.3, the remaining piece of the puzzle is an organizational infrastructure that matches, nudges, but also supports the creation and uses of a critical mass of outsider-insiders—and all within the existing culture. It is like building a supply chain but of people, not of parts. This means creating a chain of potential "pingers" who can generate the "pongs" necessary to transform organizations. Once you have this supply chain, you can tap into it, but first it has to be built. There is a need for vigilance; this is not a natural course of action for organizations. Building an infrastructure to develop, sustain, and effectively use outsider-insiders requires a process—a "people process" much like a production or supply chain process. In turn, the systematic use of that infrastructure develops the organizational capability for true change.

An outsider-insider support infrastructure is designed to change mental models of how an organization approaches challenges. Hence, it is important to consider the existing organizational culture in designing processes to develop and sustain a critical mass of outsider-insiders. The processes that an organization deploys to

Figure 4.3. Three Ingredients Necessary for True Change

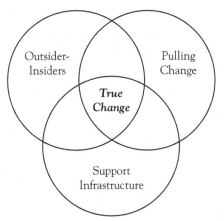

support outsider-insiders must be acceptable to current insiders while simultaneously paving the way for outsider-insiders to introduce new ideas and ways of approaching challenges that ultimately transform the culture. In other words, the support infrastructure must leverage the existing culture to change it.

In the remainder of this book, we explore four critical components to building and maintaining a critical mass of outsider-insiders throughout an organization that were introduced in Figure 1.2:

1. Developing insiders to wear two hats and learn how to apply their outsider perspectives to help overcome key organizational challenges (Chapter Five)

2. Recruiting and assimilating outsiders and helping them to build credibility as insiders without losing their outsider perspectives (Chapter Six)

3. Helping outsider-insiders get to the right place at the right time to find gaps and then help the organization pull in new ideas and concepts (Chapter Seven)

4. Ensuring that outsider-insiders keep their two hats in balance (Chapter Eight)

Throughout, we will compare and contrast two large corporations that have consciously attempted to develop and nurture outsider-insiders. One firm falls in the risk-averse category, while the other encourages new ideas but introduced according to disciplined change processes. BigFab, a traditionally risk-averse fabrication and assembly operation, built formal systems that leveraged its hierarchical, top-down culture (see Exhibit 4.1 for a profile). HiTech, in contrast, had to rely on a more informal approach using internal networks since its meritocratic policies dictated that no group is afforded special development opportunities (its profile is in Exhibit 4.2). Each developed an infrastructure that fit its unique cultural attributes. And in the end, both were successful in building a critical mass of outsider-insiders to help their respective organizations respond to a changing competitive environment.[4] This was in stark contrast to many of the other companies we studied that failed to align their support systems to their existing cultural norms. And as we will see, once a cadre of outsider-insiders is built, they become the people who nurture future developing outsider-insiders and help them to learn to wear and use two hats. It becomes a reinforcing cycle that builds and refreshes an organization's change capability so that there will be an ample supply of outsider-insiders ready to use their outsider perspectives whenever challenges arise that require true change to be pulled into the organization.

Exhibit 4.1. Profile of BigFab

BigFab employs over seventy-six thousand employees worldwide. By most accounts, it is a stereotypical traditional, risk-averse culture that reflects the nature of its industry and its product, both built up from the military-industrial complex. Given the highly integrated nature of its product line, there is a recognition (and fear) that any process change can inadvertently have negative effects on the product. In addition, because the product is a highly integrated system, there is an overriding assumption that change must come from the top of the organization. It is presumed that only senior management has the vision and ability to change the system, whether the changes be technical or organizational. Furthermore, although the organization is attempting to transform itself, strong functional fiefdoms continue to discourage cross-functional assignments.

Seniority plays a major part in all aspects of the organization, ranging from promotions to decision making and influence. This is as true in management as on the shop floor. Hence, BigFab does not readily welcome outside perspectives, especially from the younger generation. As we will see, building a critical mass of outsider-insiders requires strong intervention by influential, senior-level champions. High-level sponsors are used to strategically slot outsider-insiders in positions where traditional mind-sets are blocking achievement of strategic objectives. These sponsors and coaches tend to be influential power brokers who act as talent agents and often select opportunities for their protégés.

Exhibit 4.2. Profile of HiTech

HiTech experienced rapid growth in the early 1990s, with revenues growing by over 50 percent annually. The company's founders embedded a set of values and beliefs about how the company should operate that became ingrained in strong cultural norms. Underlying the corporate values are key assumptions about how the organization should function and what is important; for example, the organization thrives on technical people who make data-driven decisions, and recognition is results based.

HiTech's industry is still in its infancy, and there is a closely knit group of people who have worked together to build the company. Although the company has grown into a multinational business, the operation is still run on relationships. With success and growth, senior management has attempted to replicate its modes of interaction on a larger scale with formalized networks. Possibly due to this rapid pace of growth, these networks have become the common mode for communications and information sharing, and they are critical to one's success. Without a network, people have no way of quickly knowing what is happening.

An outgrowth of the technocratic culture is a belief that performance can be measured quantitatively and fairly. As such, the company has a strict peer evaluation process. There is little preference treatment afforded hierarchical position. A clear understanding of the culture is essential for outsider-insiders to be successful as "seeds" scattered across the organization pulling in change.

HiTech's support infrastructure may appear quite unstructured, but it is grounded in strong cultural norms that help connect outsider-insiders to appropriate opportunities where they can help their organization avoid cultural blind spots. Since HiTech's culture eschews any form of formal mentoring, most outsider-insiders have personal advisers who act as behind-the-scenes godparents to open doors or alert them to potential opportunities that could use alternative perspectives.

Chapter Five

Preparing Insiders to Wear Two Hats

As we noted in Chapter One and show again here in Figure 5.1, becoming outsider-insiders from within can be triggered in two ways. A challenge can cause insiders to question internal assumptions and lead them to discover a gap between their current assumptions and the root cause of that challenge, as when Ginger saw the boat was moving backward, or exposure to alternative perspectives enables insiders to examine their own assumptions. While the first more or less happens, the second one can and must be managed. Exposure to external points of view is no guarantee that insiders will automatically recognize or internalize outsider perspectives, much less seek out opportunities for pulling in change. Some people may simply go along for the ride and remain thoroughbred insiders. Hence, an organization that wants to develop a critical mass of outsider-insiders needs processes to help insiders look beyond their cultural blinders.

Wearing two hats requires an ability to simultaneously see current as well as alternative ways of doing things *and* understand the underlying assumptions that are the context for each set of practices. It's the latter—understanding the context for each approach—that sets outsider-insiders apart from insiders who just try to copy an outsider perspective without grasping whether it is truly addressing the root cause of a challenge they face.

Consider the case of an American industrial engineer who was visiting a Japanese transplant operation to learn about lean manufacturing. As she walked around the factory floor, she observed

Figure 5.1. Learning to Wear Two Hats

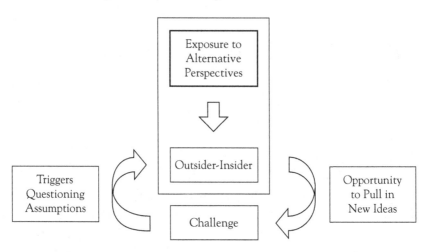

employees following standardized work practices that were illustrated in large diagrams above each workstation. At the end of the day, she remarked that the operation had just taken scientific management, that is, determining the one best method that workers should follow, to a new height. At that moment, her Japanese "tour guide" rebutted her statement with a stern scolding: "You are looking at the work flow through Western eyes!" What she had missed was that the system was dynamic, with production employees continuously improving the work flow through a disciplined process rather than just engineers dictating the one best method. She had observed an artifact, standardized work charts, and then used her prior assumptions to interpret how the work standards had been developed. She had failed to let go of her previous cultural assumptions to be open to looking at both the content (standardized work charts) and the context (cultural assumptions around continuous improvement and discipline). Fortunately, she had a coach who proactively helped her to see past her cultural blinders.

Becoming an outsider-insider from within an organization is in many respects a personal development journey. It is about learning one's own deeply engrained insider assumptions and then being open to question those beliefs. All too often, new mental models end up being an unintended consequence, rather than an expected outcome, of exposure to alternative perspectives.[1] When they are not planned for or valued, the two hats tend to get put on the shelf and not worn to help solve organizational challenges. Furthermore, many new "two hatters" become frustrated and disenchanted when their peers and supervisors appear uninterested in alternative ways to improve organizational performance. This chapter focuses on creating an infrastructure comprising robust processes that provide insiders with opportunities to be exposed to alternative perspectives and then support them in learning how to use their insider and outsider perspectives simultaneously to find opportunities to pull in new ideas. As we will see, the journey requires the combined energies of insiders and their organizations working together to set the stage for their role in true change.

Learning to Wear Two Hats

One can pick up new ideas in many different ways—for example, by reading a book or watching a movie and passively learning about alternative perspectives, interacting with consultants or trainers who are brought in from the outside to help solve problems or build new internal competencies, or attending a seminar or class on new tools or methodologies. All of these represent exposure to alternative perspectives, but they do not necessarily lead to questioning of existing assumptions.

Insiders can truly understand what's going on in the outside world only if they are willing to let go of their existing assumptions and look through the eyes of other outsiders. Like the industrial engineer learning about lean manufacturing, they can easily miss essential clues if they don't understand the external environment's assumptions. But there is also a danger in going to the other extreme: "going native" and throwing away all prior assumptions while learning about the new environment. Although it may appear easier to cut off the old while learning the new, insiders who choose to go that way often just accept external norms without examining what's different in internal versus external assumptions that lead to specific behaviors. In essence, they go from being an insider in one environment to an insider in another. Wearing two hats, by comparison, means simultaneously exploring two different sets of underlying assumptions about how one goes about doing things. It is not a sequential process.

There are numerous opportunities to interact with external environments and learn about outsider perspectives as part of one's regular job duties. But unfortunately, these activities are not recognized or capitalized on as a chance to develop outsider perspectives. Being a member of a dispersed team is a perfect example. Members can just show up, contribute their technical or functional expertise, and return to the rest of their job untainted by any outsider viewpoint. This is a missed opportunity. A global or multidisciplinary team provides a window to the outside to learn about new ideas and concepts and to have others test local assumptions. Through dialogue with remote team members, insiders often learn how their assumptions might be contributing to the root problem of a particular challenge or a missed opportunity for continuous improvement. Hence, being in a matrixed team, whether global or multidisciplinary, provides an opportunity to learn to wear two hats simultaneously.[2]

By moving out of one's cultural environment either physically or virtually (for example, on a globally dispersed team), one's mental models are altered, and gaps between current assumptions and alternative models get identified. Insiders do not have to pack up and leave their workplaces to pick up outsider perspectives. With the right mind-set and support, becoming an outsider-insider can become a planned by-product of carrying out a work assignment. Although it may seem more difficult or less likely to break out of mental models while still encased within a work setting, it is possible. As we will see, with proper expectations and a supportive infrastructure, daily opportunities, such as being a member of a multidisciplinary or globally dispersed team, provide windows to outsider perspectives.

Another way to learn to wear two hats is through total immersion outside one's normal workplace. This might be an assignment overseas as an expatriate or being physically moved into a cross-functional role (in other words, relocated to a totally new function). Both surround an individual in an unfamiliar environment where customs and assumptions are typically different from those at one's home base. In such situations, insiders become outsiders in their new work setting. In addition to learning about the new milieu, contradictions between prior assumptions and those held by new associates force the examination of one's own mental models. Leaving one's workplace to attend a full-time educational program serves a similar purpose. Beyond learning new skills and competencies, one is surrounded by people from different organizations or nations. As one returning outsider-insider noted, "One lives in one's own small world, so going back to school opens one's eyes." This recognition that there are multiple ways to look at a situation is the first step in learning to wear two hats.

Not every employee has the interest or capability to become a proactive outsider-insider who finds opportunities to pull in change, but many do. Those who are inclined to become outsider-insiders are untapped resources to help their organizations transform themselves from the inside. Hence, we begin this chapter by exploring two types of developmental activities that can help insiders learn to wear two hats: (1) windows to the outside that are part of, or parallel to, one's daily job and (2) total immersion in a "foreign culture." They are alternative paths, each with its own set of pros and cons. In the end, both can be equally effective provided an infrastructure is created to support the insiders on their journey to becoming outsider-insiders, the topic we turn to at the end of the chapter.

A Window to the Outside: Becoming Outsiders While Still on the Inside

The main roadblock to becoming an outsider-insider while still on the inside is time. Everyone's job duties are so jam-packed that there is rarely enough time to step back and reflect on either internal or external perspectives. Learning about outside cultural assumptions takes time. Many multidisciplinary and globally dispersed teams fail because their team members try to short-circuit the process of getting to understand each other's perspectives. There is often an assumption that the work of the team will override any cultural differences. But that is rarely the case, except in very narrowly defined technical or emergency situations.[3]

Another problem is what I call dirty windows cluttered with cultural cobwebs. A combination of "not invented here," "it doesn't apply to my situation," and "there is no way I could sell that" contributes to a perceived resistance to clearing the cobwebs. And since there is no clear break from daily internal priorities and pressures, insiders get only a periodic and truncated glimpse of the outside. In many cases, windows get partially opened and then slammed shut by supervisors, managers, or peers who are demanding immediate attention to local tasks. As a result, insiders must have a personal inclination, and their organizations must consciously plan to keep windows open and cleaned. That's part of the needed infrastructure to help insiders learn to wear two hats.

In a study of globally dispersed teams, members of one of the most successful teams found themselves being penalized on their performance reviews by local supervisors, who felt they were spending too much time on global rather than local duties.[4] The team members recognized the importance of learning from one another and saw an opportunity to use their new outsider perspectives to suggest improvements to their home operations. Although they paid a short-term personal price, their efforts eventually paid off when the team was recognized through a corporate award program as an outstanding benchmark for sharing across borders. In this case, the team members learned how to wear two hats and found opportunities to pull in change despite a lack of support from their immediate hierarchy. Their success was totally personality driven, in other words, happenstance based on the personal drive of the individual team members. Their organization failed them and, worse yet, had no way to replicate their success. A supportive organization, especially at a local level, is essential for insiders to find time and space—two necessary conditions—to explore alternative perspectives for becoming outsider-insiders from within.

Everyone thinks they have an open mind, but then the hidden cobwebs or unconscious mental models sneak in. A little voice speaks up and says, "That's an interesting idea, but it just doesn't apply here." The longer one has been an insider, the more entrenched those hidden assumptions tend to be: years of socialization lead to unexamined habits and routines. Clearing away the cobwebs requires a frontal assault on these existing cultural assumptions. It requires a willingness to suspend current assumptions, at least temporarily to open one's mind to what is being witnessed, something the industrial engineer visiting the Japanese transplant failed to do, for instance.

Some people are able to uncover their unexamined assumptions on their own, but most need assistance to explore potentially new mental models. That's the role the Japanese tour guide played for the industrial engineer. Feedback from others acts as a mirror to reveal personal cobwebs. Hence, dialogue with others creates an opportunity to explore how outsider perspectives might apply to internal organizational challenges. The absence of feedback from "tour guides" can lead to missed signals or flawed interpretations of observations.

When one is immersed on the outside, the external environment typically provides the stimulus or jolt to question one's assumptions, but insiders on the inside who are merely looking through a window often need additional stimulus. Insiders need peers who are willing to ask tough questions and be a devil's advocate—someone to push back and dig below the surface. It helps to have several insiders making the journey together. This way, peers act as outsider coaches to each other and explore alternative approaches through open dialogue.

Strong cohorts, on both the inside and the outside, can be both a blessing and a curse, however. When cohorts are too homogeneous, peer influence can lead to groupthink. Some groups tend to ostracize members who question norms or routines, especially when time is at a premium to accomplish a task. Individuals can be so concerned about fitting in that they become leery of questioning one another. This occurred during a teleconference of technical experts when engineers at one site looked at each other when the microphone was muted and said, "What a stupid thing to say."[5] When an observer asked them why they didn't voice their opinion to the remote team member, one of the engineers noted, "It would be an insult to question a fellow engineer's expertise." Here, the cobwebs—assumptions concerning professional and cross-cultural protocols—ended up clouding the window. The engineers did not want to make a colleague look stupid, and there was no opportunity to take the remote engineer aside in a private conversation to question his analysis. Fortunately, the observer acted as an outsider to help the group see where their cultural assumptions were inhibiting a free flow of ideas.

Since interaction with the outside world is often done by telecommunication, becoming an outsider while still at home requires learning to look through a virtual window. Learning to see what outsiders perceive depends on the degree to which insiders are able to create a virtual presence. This is feeling as if you are somewhere else without really being there, for example, being on a telephone call, hearing a voice, and imagining the expression on the caller's face. It is also what makes computer simulations seem real. In both cases, people are able to suspend their assumptions of time and space and experience the sensation of virtually being in another environment. It is being able to be in both places—"here" and "there," that is, on the inside and the outside simultaneously—and getting the understanding of what differences can be harvested.

Obviously, a key ingredient for creating a virtual presence is the communication technology to provide a seamless interface. But technology alone will not create a virtual presence if cultural cobwebs cloud the view. For example, many organizations tend to be headquarters-centric. As a result, remote locations are only half heard, and even when they do get a chance to voice their opinion, the dominance of influence at headquarters discounts the value of alternative perspectives. In these cases, individuals at remote sites may very well experience a virtual presence with headquarters, but the cobwebs are as bad as intermittent technological disruptions in blocking what is heard and understood at headquarters. In other words, cobwebs will persist even in the presence of sophisticated technology if cultural assumptions are not broken down.

A shortage of time also leads many employees to multitask during virtual interactions. They mute their speakerphone and talk to local peers or read their e-mail, for example. Despite the presumed efficiency associated with accomplishing two tasks at once, one's mindshare (the distribution of one's attention applied to specific activities) gets distracted from the virtual experience.[6] When this happens, virtual presence diminishes. Multitasking, even with an open mind, leads to missed clues and only half-hearing what's happening on the outside.

In a survey of engineers participating in distance-learning classes, respondents noted that they could more easily apply what they were learning while on the job but were unable to question their own assumptions at a distance. On the surface, this seems contradictory, since learning usually involves questioning assumptions. That is true for learning new concepts or ways of thinking but not necessarily a requirement for learning new technical tools or methodologies that are often just plugged into current work assumptions. In other words, the engineers readily found opportunities to apply those tools that fit into their current mental models but tuned out, and probably multitasked on other activities, when "foreign" concepts were discussed. As well, the peer coaching necessary to help insiders question their assumptions is often lacking in virtual settings, as evidenced by the engineer who was unwilling to question his distant colleague. Many of these discussions tend to occur on an informal basis walking between classes (or meetings in a work-related setting) and over lunch or a beer at the end of the day.

Given the inherent difficulties in breaking away from the daily grind to explore alternative perspectives, many insiders striving to learn how to wear two hats will, when given the opportunity, opt for full immersion. It provides time and space away from the daily pressures of one's home environment to reflect and see the world in a different way. Although this may appear to be a panacea, there are also risks associated with being out of sight, out of mind.

Total Immersion: Insiders on the Outside

By moving out of their existing work environment, insiders are thrust into a totally foreign culture. They, in essence, become *insiders* on the outside, but in actuality they are now outsiders to the outside world they are visiting because they have yet to learn the new environment they have entered. While the distinction between inside and outside depends on one's orientation, the fact remains that they have left their home environment and have been thrust into a totally different culture. Obviously, the farther that insiders stray, the bigger the cultural gap is bound to be.

Even when the move is across fairly permeable boundaries, stepping outside amplifies distinctions between the inside and the outside. Going outside means leaving peer groups behind and becoming a newcomer to another group. As we will see in the next chapter, that requires learning the ropes, understanding new norms and routines, and building credibility as an insider to the new group. It also means learning a new language, even if it is just new acronyms or the jargon used by another function. Given enough time, insiders on the outside can become outsider-insiders in their new environment provided they have not "gone native" and forgotten the experiences and assumptions that they brought with them from home. This gives them practice in wearing two hats even before returning home.

Time and distance tend to accentuate the unintended consequences of full-immersion development activities and can easily lead to a mismatch of expectations between developing outsider-insiders and their organizations about how their new perspectives will, or will not, be used. Take Pete, for example. He decided to go back to school to get his "ticket punched, but what I really got was the idea of how good things can be. It really opened my eyes to the world." Since his company had sponsored his two years of schooling, he assumed that his organization was looking to him to apply what he learned. He returned pumped up, ready to pass along his new outsider perspectives. Pete's energy and aspiration to apply new ideas, however, quickly turned to disappointment when he perceived that no one was interested. He eventually concluded that fitting back into the old culture was easier than the uphill battle to try to change things. As Pete described:

> When I came out of school I was just bursting with ideas. You just see the low-hanging fruit everywhere. . . . I tried every possible way to get people to think outside the box. Most of the time, all I got was the glazed-eye syndrome. People just did not understand the concepts. The thing that was so disheartening was their lack of comprehension. . . . So I said, what the hell, I'll just write a newsletter. I did it four or five times. I got no positive feedback, and I got busy with other things and have let my expectations slip. Sometimes you're happier when you don't know. Ignorance is bliss. I was fairly ignorant before I went back to school. Now I see. I am more responsible now and perhaps not as happy.

Pete's discontent continued to deepen, and after five years he left to work for another organization where he believed his ideas would be better used.

Unfortunately, Pete's story is not an anomaly. Returning expatriates face similar disinterest in their new insights and ideas. One study showed that 25 percent of employees who return from overseas assignments leave their companies within the first year, and this doesn't count those who didn't return at the end of their assignments.[7] This is especially troublesome since these are typically people who already have credibility internally based on their prior successes within their companies. They are recognized insiders who understand the culture and are prime candidates for finding opportunities to pull in alternative ways of doing things. Their organizations have made significant investments to support their development and are now missing out on building on their experiences and using their new perspectives to help change parochial views of the world.

Part of the problem is that newly minted outsider-insiders do not look any different than they did when they were insiders, but their mental models of the world have changed dramatically.

Conveying this change in one's point of view to former peers is often difficult. As one returning outsider-insider recalled, "I was probably having an identity crisis. I had just spent two years at school and had different views on things and had expanded the way I looked at the world. People at my site were looking at me as if I had never left." This individual may have picked up outsider perspectives but had yet to learn how to wear and use two hats simultaneously.

Although insiders learning to wear two hats while staying planted within the culture experience similar identity crises, it tends to occur more slowly, and they have more opportunities to share new perspectives with their coworkers gradually. For employees who have gone the full-immersion route, reentry into the home culture is a stark reminder of the old mental models. To complicate matters, most organizations are not prepared for properly using new outsider-insiders. As one manager observed,

> I don't think the organization knows what to do with them. They are an anomaly. Others have never been there themselves and they do not know what to do with them when they return. The way I think about it is like if you are from a family that grows up in the middle of Minnesota and have never traveled. Their kids go away and come back, and people don't understand or appreciate what they have seen. There is an attempt to assimilate them back into the culture. What do you do with these people?

This lack of clarity around who one is and what the organization should "do with these people" typically frustrates new outsider-insiders. Worse, their managers and peers often label them as misfits if they start to push their new perspectives onto others. Hence, organizations and developing outsider-insiders must plan each step of the journey. For organizations, this means creating support infrastructures that start before the development activity itself. It should begin with the selection criteria and process for identifying insiders who have the potential to wear two hats, which clearly sets expectations for the entire organization (aligning the organization around a macro challenge). It continues throughout the development process by providing linkages between the inside and outside and offering help in finding assignments that will maximize the opportunities to apply newly acquired skills and knowledge to finding gaps. And as we will see, this process is a two-way street: both the organization and the developing outsider-insider take a proactive stance in using the infrastructure.

Building an Infrastructure to Support Insiders Learning to Wear Two Hats

Some organizations do a better job than others in managing development activities to better use insiders who learn to wear two hats. In our study of twelve organizations that sponsored talented young employees to return for advanced degrees, there was a wide variability in retention and use of returning graduates.[8] For example, retention rates within each company ranged from 100 percent to 0 percent over a five-year period. Not surprisingly, the organizations that were most successful in retaining and using their newly developed outsider-insiders provided an organizational infrastructure to support their insiders throughout the development journey.

We found a similar story in a parallel study of organizations that funded insiders to participate in a two-year distance education program. Support infrastructures for these insiders becoming outsider-insiders while still surrounded by internal demands and mental models include many of the same system elements that are needed for successful full immersion, for example, identifying insiders for on-the-job development activities and setting clear expectations on how outside perspectives can be used internally to help overcome challenges at hand. In many respects, clearly articulating the macro challenges where outsider perspectives are immediately required is even more critical since local priorities tend to drag insiders away from open windows. Although insiders might appear to be peering outside, their minds are often on the pile of other tasks building up on their to-do lists. Hence, developing outsider-insiders

need support from their organizations to help their immediate supervisors and peers recognize the value of their development activities.

In most respects, the infrastructures that organizations use for
looking through the window and full immersion can and should be
one and the same. Since the two paths are complementary and both
create outsider-insiders who look the same postdevelopment, it is
optimal to have integrated infrastructures. This is not a situation
where one path is better than the other; both are important and
should be encouraged to create a critical mass of outsider-insiders.
Furthermore, many individual outsider-insiders may journey along
both paths at different points in their career.

Finding opportunities to pull external views and ideas into an
organization requires a partnership between outsider-insiders and
their organizations, that is, managers and supervisors. Individuals
obviously must manage their own destiny, including making sure
they are exposed to appropriate developmental activities and then
building credibility for their ideas. Yet their managers have a responsibility to help guide career opportunities and break down systemic
barriers that may hinder finding opportunities to pull in outsider
ideas that align with where the organization wants to be. The objective is to transform the random acts of luck into predictable events
that place outsider-insiders in the right place at the right time to pull
in their new perspectives. As we will see in Chapter Seven, this
requires middle-level managers and supervisors who understand the
value of, and in many cases are themselves, outsider-insiders.

An organization's support system architecture must be designed
to negotiate a fine line between conforming to cultural norms while
providing a platform for outsider-insiders to act in nontraditional
ways. Not surprisingly, these factors are much like the ones identified for successful repatriation of employees returning from overseas assignments: setting expectations, maintaining linkages while
abroad, and early planning around reentry strategies.[9] We will explore
these aspects individually and then use the best practice case studies
of BigFab and HiTech to illustrate how they fit together to create
an integrated infrastructure that both conforms to and nudges the

existing culture and enables an organization to create a critical mass of outsider-insiders.

Identifying Insiders for Outsider-Insider Development Activities

Deciding to venture into the outside world can be a significant risk for an insider. Many developing outsider-insiders who stay on the inside worry about being ostracized for taking time away from current duties to learn about outsider perspectives and being viewed as someone "rattling the cages" when they try to share what they learned. For those who choose to go the full-immersion route, it can mean relocating to another city or country and worrying about whether there will be a reentry opportunity that is as good as (or better than) the position one left. Similarly, the organization is taking a chance that insiders selected for development activities will in fact succeed in helping others to see alternative perspectives. There can also be significant tangible costs associated with the journey outside, such as training or tuition costs and relocation expenses. Hence, the process for identifying insiders with the desire and potential to wear two hats should be as critical a decision as deciding whether to invest in capital equipment. And like a capital investment, it should have an expected return on investment that includes where and how that investment will be used.

The process and criteria used for selection send a message to both those who are selected and the rest of the organization about the value placed on developing outsider-insiders. Regardless of the existing organizational culture, two factors appear to be universal truths: (1) the investment in external development activities should be tied to a macro challenge, and (2) the selection criteria must be clearly articulated. Remember Pete who decided to go back to school to get his ticket punched and returned to find that no one cared what he had learned? Since his decision to go back to school was totally self-initiated, there was no articulated organizational challenge for his outsider perspectives to match. He was unable to convince others that his ideas on how to improve the operation were of value, and the organization eventually lost a valuable contributor.

As a counterpoint, let's look at Charlie's experience in trying to make similar changes after reentry to an equally risk-averse company. Charlie had worked in a number of factories and built significant credibility for his ability to deliver results. His mentor suggested he go back to school for advanced training in manufacturing since there was a critical shortage of people to help his organization make a transition to a lean structure and culture. As Charlie recalled, "My mentor steered me. He was looking for people who had high potential in manufacturing. He wanted to have them help change manufacturing in its conversion from mass to lean production. There is a lack of talent at the plant level."

By clearly articulating why Charlie was selected for development activities, he had a better idea of where to look for outsider perspectives that would help his organization achieve its strategic objectives. Furthermore, Charlie had a launchpad ready for him on return: the macro challenge provided an opportunity for him to use his outsider perspectives to address micro workplace challenges, or what Pete referred to as "low-hanging fruit."

Macro challenges also help to identify the selection criteria. If, for example, the intent is to diffuse corporate values and practices to satellite locations around the globe, the criteria for selecting insiders to go on overseas assignments would include the ability to teach ideas to diverse constituencies. If, however, the goal is to fix a technical problem, the selection would be based on product or process expertise. But in both cases, newly developed outsider-insiders will want to share their new points of view when they return. Hence, to avoid a situation similar to Pete's, other criteria should include the potential for individuals to learn how to wear two hats and have the organizational credibility to use their outsider hats to help solve challenges. Key characteristics to look for would include an ability to see nuances and understand human behavior, such as digging below the surface as to why people behave as they do. This is often evident by the degree to which an individual asks probing questions or considers multiple stakeholder perspectives.

Maintaining Linkages

People who are developing outsider-insiders need to be continually reminded of the macro challenges facing their organizations. There are many possible outsider perspectives that insiders will be exposed to during their development journey. They need someone, such as Charlie's mentor, to help steer them to develop perspectives that will be useful internally. Often this role is played by outsider-insiders who have already experienced the journey. Not only do they tend to be more sensitive to the trials and tribulations associated with learning to wear two hats, they already value outsider perspectives.

Many companies attempt to provide the linkages, but these are often not embedded in the culture or buttressed by pre- and post-support actions, that is, not considered an integral part of the i nfrastructure. Rather, such ties are usually just a result of an individual's personality and the initiative of a mentor. This scattershot approach can lead to accusations of favoritism and comparisons between the haves and the have-nots—in other words, those who have good linkages and those who do not. But the responsibility for maintaining linkages rests as much with developing outsider-insiders as with their organization. Ultimately, these people are the ones who must either encourage or ignore communications from home. This is particularly true in meritocratic cultures, where employees are responsible for managing their own networks.

The need to remain connected is especially keen for insiders who are fully immersed on the outside. The linkages must give distant employees sufficient autonomy to experience and absorb their new cultural environments while making them feel that someone back home still remembers them. If the bonds are too tight, there is a risk that one will not break out of the mental models that block absorption of new ideas or be willing to explore alternative worldviews. Linkages also serve as a conduit for letting home sponsors or peers have a window into what insiders are learning on the outside. Without periodic communications, insiders run a risk of being viewed as just someone who was away "on vacation" and not providing value to the organization. As one returning outsider-insider lamented, "It was sort of the mentality of 'you never really changed, and what you did didn't make sense.' They didn't see me as having new skills. . . . In retrospect, it would have been better to enter anew, and not have to overcome previous exposure and preconceptions."

The scenario might have been quite different if his organization had done a better job, as in Charlie's case, of aligning his development activities to a pull at either a macro or micro level. Yet returning employees do own a major part of the responsibility for maintaining the linkages. Hence, this painful return could have been avoided if the insider had recognized he shared the responsibility for maintaining linkages and educating his peer group on what he was learning and how it differed from his previous exposure and assumptions. The story was quite different for another particularly astute insider on the outside within the same company who recognized that she needed to illustrate the relevance of her development experience to key supporters she left behind. Doing so was especially important because the organization was undergoing a major restructuring. She recalled,

> I didn't have a mentor, but had an ad hoc group of people who supported my going back to school. With so many things changing, I realized that I needed to have more than one sponsor. I promised to keep in touch with each person. . . . There really isn't a before and after school for me since I kept up an ongoing dialogue. It was really a small amount of work for me. If I wrote a paper for a course, I would shoot it off to someone. You have to make an effort to keep the network going.

Maintaining linkages back home, as this outsider-insider did, also eases the transition or reentry process upon return from full-immersion development activities. With open communication channels, outsider-insiders bridge the two worlds by being periodically reminded of their internal assumptions as well as keeping abreast of home developments because things usually change while insiders are away in full-immersion development activities. People often fear being forgotten while on the outside, even if the outside is only a different functional group. Upon return, the connections begin to create a network of people to help with the process of finding a good job match, to put the new outsider perspectives to work, and to help solve an important or urgent challenge.

Managing Expectations

The mere fact that only a small fraction of the workforce is selected for development opportunities naturally raises these people's expectations that the organization plans to use their new skills and knowledge (remember Pete's disappointment when he learned that wasn't necessarily the case). As we have also seen, there is a risk of bifurcating the workforce between those who are selected for development activities and those who are not. Unless expectations are carefully managed, a mismatch in expectations on the part of both groups is highly likely.

With a never-ending stream of mergers, acquisitions, and corporate restructurings, setting clear expectations among all stakeholders is a continual struggle since many key players change before employees complete their developmental assignments. Once again, this is particularly problematic for insiders who decide to go on full-immersion tours of duty. Since many returning outsider-insiders find a totally transformed, and often streamlined, organization upon their return, there is a need to both set initial expectations and manage changes that occur due to an evolving environmental landscape. For example, one organization required any candidate being considered for full immersion on the outside to develop comprehensive reentry plans. But even the best-laid plans can go awry. For one unfortunate returnee, the economy changed, and his organization was drastically downsized:

> As part of the interview process with the executive selection committee, I had to lay out what my reentry points would be. Who would I contact when I returned? It was tough to project out two

years ahead, but I had to articulate all of that—who I would contact, when, what jobs I would be looking for, etc. . . . In terms of the
four areas I thought I'd go to, one plant was sold, the other plant was
part of a company that was sold, and the third (the group I was in
before I left) had been brought down from 220 to 20 people. Only
one of the four was intact. The net result was that the choices open
to me to go into my desired roles were gone because the company
had sold plants and downsized significantly.

This individual's experience highlights the need to manage initial expectations *and* changes in those expectations on the part of
both the organization and the developing outsider-insider. Even in
organizations that have not gone through major restructuring,
many sponsors move on and are not in a position to help returning
outsider-insiders through the reentry process.

In addition, in companies where the technology is rapidly
changing, two years can mean a total leap in product technology.
As one returnee discovered, nontechnical developmental opportunities can detract from developing and maintaining technical
expertise, especially in technocratic organizations: "When I came
back, I was probably less skilled [technically]. I didn't have the subject area expertise that others did." Furthermore, former peers who
stayed on the job rather than "disappearing" for a couple of years
often found promotional opportunities that moved them ahead in
their careers. As one newly minted outsider-insider noted, "When
I came back, some of my peers that I was working with before were
higher up. It just took awhile to realize that I knew I had a better
outlook. It wasn't that long, about six months, but it was still long
enough to feel like a victim."

Although this individual, like most other developing outsider-
insiders, caught up quickly, perceived disparities can lead to short-
term consternation. Feelings of inequity or sacrifice may also limit
and distract developing outsider-insiders. They become worried
about what they are missing rather than learning about the outside
world and how they might use what they learn when they return.

Overinflated expectations are particularly troublesome in organizations where employees nominate themselves for development
activities. Although many hope that advanced degrees or other
development activities will be their ticket to success, there is no
guarantee they will magically become high-potential employees
when they return. As a result, emphasizing that those selected for .
development activities are "the chosen few" to lead the company
when they return is sure to backfire. As one returning outsider-
insider who was on the verge of leaving his company because he
didn't feel his organization had delivered on its implied promises
put it, "There is this big conference in June for all the sponsored
fellows. They talk about how important it is to mentor the future
leaders of the company. There is a lot of trust building and HR feel-
good stuff. They tell you that you will be leaders of the company
and they give all kinds of statistics about former sponsored fellows.
They make you feel honored to be one. They said that we would be
shepherded through the organization."

Newly minted outsider-insiders can also face overinflated expectations and comments from peers and managers about how they are
expected to save the organization now that they have been exposed
to outside ideas. As one recalled, "Many people expect you to walk
on water. Managers make a big splash about you, so the expectations
are quite high." This just sets newly developed outsider-insiders
up for a letdown when it is discovered that they are not miracle
workers.

As we have seen, stakeholder alignment is critical in creating
a receptive environment for change. This means that clear expectations among managers and employees up and down the hierarchy must be set around the roles outsider-insiders are expected
to play, especially relative to their responsibility in helping to
introduce new ideas into their organizations. Without a clearly
articulated strategic pull, those who are selected for choice development activities face significant peer resistance. In addition, the
expectations of recently developed outsider-insiders need to be aligned
with what is feasible given the existing organizational culture.

Returning Home from Full Immersion

If the infrastructure has worked up to this point, reentry from full immersion outside can be fairly painless. Midwest's placement of newly developed outsider-insiders into the Lean University made it clear to all that their role was to help teach and diffuse the knowledge they gained while on the outside. There was a clear macro challenge and a strategy in place to use employees returning from a two-year development assignment to kick-start the organization's transformation to lean. The strategy also fit Midwest's existing hierarchical culture: the returning outsider-insiders were staff assistants to the vice president. They had the authorization of an influential champion and a knowledge transfer platform that cascaded down the hierarchy. In many respects, however, it became a way station. Once the new outsider-insiders had completed their staff assignment, they had to find an appropriate line position where they could begin to demonstrate the value of their outsider ideas at a micro level. Fortunately, they had their prior network, plus new contacts developed while part of the Lean University, as well as an influential sponsor to help in reentry. The processes worked well for Midwest, but it was very situation and sponsor dependent.

Midwest's approach would not work in a meritocratic organization where the cultural expectation is to find your own job. But when outsider-insiders in entrepreneurial companies compare notes with peers in more hierarchical organizations, they sometimes feel betrayed by their organization for not providing a more paternalistic infrastructure. One recently minted outsider-insider in an entrepreneurial company complained, "There was no consideration as to finding a job where I could utilize what I had learned." Another lamented, "It was as if the company as a whole sent you out, but there was no investment or mechanism to bring us back in." What these individuals failed to recognize was that they owned the responsibility to manage their reentry process because that was the cultural norm within their company. In these cases, the mismatch was between individual and organizational expectations rather than a lack of an infrastructure.

With the right mind-set and a bit of planning, proactive outsider-insiders can use the reentry process to begin building a critical mass of understanding, and hopefully support, for new concepts. For example, one enterprising returnee saw the reentry job search as a prime opportunity and set up forty-minute meetings with key managers to communicate what he had learned. He then condensed his outsider insights so that busy managers would be able to take them in. As he described, "I was both trying to get a job for myself and to tell people what I had learned. The first twenty minutes was my personal pitch, and then I told them about what I had learned, information they could often use. I said to my interviewers, 'The reason I'm here is to share with you what I learned.' That latter part went exceedingly well. The interviews were also a mechanism to get new knowledge about my own company."

This example illustrates how an entrepreneurial stance, especially in an entrepreneurial company, can begin the ball rolling for future support and, given the culture of the organization, is what was needed for successful reentry. But regardless of the culture, the reentry interview process provides a mechanism to broaden networks for the future and to begin building support for outsider perspectives. At this point the newly created outsider-insiders are ready to begin looking for opportunities to pull in change, the topic we turn to in Chapter Seven.

Two Contrasting Support Infrastructures

Designing support structures for preparing insiders to wear two hats is a systemic process. Not only do the pieces of the infrastructure need to fit together, they also need to be accepted by the existing culture. BigFab and HiTech provide contrasting best practice cases to illustrate how a comprehensive system might look in two very different cultural environments. Both companies had a business need, or macro challenge, to develop outsider-insiders. Although each had different challenges, they turned to similar full-immersion development activities, a two-year educational program, to create a critical mass of outsider-insiders to help find micro-level opportunities to transform their operations.

BigFab faced increasingly fierce worldwide competition that forced cost reductions that it could achieve only if manufacturing people and product development people worked together. But like Niche Manufacturing, both status and skill differentiations created a chasm between the two functions. Historically, the product development function was the kingpin in all decision making, with manufacturing a distant second- or third-class citizen. The strategy chosen to respond to the challenge was to infuse high-caliber engineering talent into the manufacturing organization in an effort to upgrade operational skills and level the playing field. Because new people were perceived to have difficulty assimilating into the culture and the product development group was a very technocratic group that valued only engineering expertise, BigFab decided to take a small number of its own technical experts, educate them in how to run operations, and then strategically place them within the manufacturing operations. The intent was to create a group of technical peers within operations who could stand on an equal footing with the product development group.

HiTech's situation was quite different. Rather than facing a potentially contracting market share, it was having difficulty finding enough capacity to meet customer needs. Although the manufacturing leaders were all engineers, they lacked a world-class manufacturing mentality and skill set; they preferred to tinker with the product design rather than build a robust manufacturing process. As a result, the corporation decided to take some of its best and brightest and send them to an advanced educational program focused on manufacturing. Their role was to instill manufacturing disciplines at the shop floor level after they returned.

Both companies faced some early hurdles in clarifying expectations; for example, some of the returning newly developed outsider-insiders had overinflated expectations, and many of the insiders resented their being identified as implementers of new ideas. Yet they were able to quickly adjust and create an integrated support infrastructure for developing outsider-insiders. Both companies recognized that they needed to clearly articulate their respective macro challenges and the roles that these newly developed outsider-insiders were to play. Because their development was tied to a strategic objective, it became a bit more palatable for insiders who were not selected for similar development activities. At least they now knew what they needed to do if they wanted to be eligible for similar development opportunities.

When it came to selecting potential candidates, BigFab and HiTech developed processes that fit their respective cultures. Although both involved senior-level review, each step of the process was tailored to internal norms. At BigFab, individuals were tapped and presented with the opportunity. One of BigFab's outsider-insiders recalled, "I did not choose it. They chose me. My management nominated me." The pool of candidates was then reviewed by a selection committee, and the top contenders were interviewed and selected by senior vice presidents.

In contrast, HiTech insiders had to take the initiative on their own to learn and apply for development opportunities. Although managers might suggest that a candidate consider a specific development activity, employees self-nominated themselves. The pool of candidates was then reviewed by a selection committee comprising several outsider-insiders who had gone through the same educational program. Finally, each of the top finalists was required to write an essay and then argue persuasively in a ten-minute presentation to senior executives as to why HiTech should invest in his or her development. Potential candidates competed solely on their merits, regardless of who might have supported their nomination.

Part of BigFab's and HiTech's success in retaining insiders who temporarily left for full immersion on the outside is the attention that they paid to maintaining connections back home during the time away. An active support network of BigFab managers who previously went through a similar full-immersion process met quarterly and linked in developing outsider-insiders on the outside with an audioconference. Before the network was populated, a liaison was appointed to maintain frequent contact with those on the outside.

HiTech's network was more informal than BigFab's but just as active. Developing outsider-insiders frequently "checked in" with fellow employees who had preceded them in their full-immersion experience. HiTech also provided a point of contact for employees outside the organization whose job was to make sure linkages back home remained intact. As one of HiTech's managers who was assigned to be a liaison recalled, "During the two years that they were away at school, I had frequent phone contact with them. We had an 800 number and I encouraged them to call. Whenever I was on campus, which was usually every six to eight weeks, I tried to schedule one-on-one's with them."

In BigFab's case, candid discussions with executive sponsors also provide pivotal points to clarify expectations and build loyalty to the organization for employees who were sent off for full immersion on the outside. As one outsider-insider noted,

> One of the burning questions I wanted to ask my vice president before I went back to school was, "What ties me to BigFab? Do I have to come back?" His response was, "I don't expect you to come back unless we treat you right. There were no ties, we just want you to come back". . . . My expectations were pretty much the way things turned out. If they spend money on me, they should accelerate my progress, mentor me, and teach me. All those things have happened.

Even with the best support systems, the reentry process can still be a bit rocky. Recognizing potential problems, BigFab provided support for returning outsider-insiders that included managers making sure that returnees felt valued. As one executive noted, "When they come back, they have a little bit of an orphan status. They are gone for two years. Who are they? It is not easy. The manufacturing bureaucracy is tough to penetrate. They need someone to say, 'How are you doing?' They need a friend to help them." This orphan status and the need for a "father figure" is consistent with BigFab's hierarchical and authorization culture.

Not surprisingly, HiTech's processes for maintaining linkages and setting expectations for reentry were quite different. From the first day of employment at HiTech, it is made clear that one's development activities and how one's ideas or perspectives will be used is driven by individual initiative. But while HiTech's culture shuns formal sponsorship, the company does provide what it calls "godparents" to watch over developing outsider-insiders from a distance and provide guidance should they need it. Beyond that, however, insiders on the outside are left to leverage their own network to maintain linkages and find support for reentry. According to one of HiTech's returning insiders, "I was able to connect with a plant manager who gave me a job that allowed me to leverage my experience, but it was self-initiated." In other words, she was able to build on her prior connections to find a reentry point that would be friendly to outsider-insiders. Upon reentry, the only protection provided returning employees was a one-year moratorium from a peer performance ranking process to give them time to reestablish themselves. Being out of the loop for two years makes it difficult to hit the ground running at full speed due to changes in a rapidly evolving technology.

As shown in Table 5.1, the support infrastructures that emerged at BigFab and HiTech illustrate how each of the individual elements—selection of insiders for development activities, maintenance of linkages while on the development journey, clarity around how new perspectives are to be applied, reentry processes for those who went outside—is part of a mosaic that reinforces one another. Furthermore, each of the support infrastructures was tailored to their respective cultures. The result was a significant number of outsider-insiders who are now scattered across the organizations ready and willing to pull in outsider perspectives to improve their organizations. But their reentry is just the beginning of the story for setting the stage for pulling change. In Chapter Seven, we will return to the final phase of getting these newly developed outsider-insiders to the right place at the right time to use their two hats to find opportunities to pull in alternative approaches to solving challenges. But first, we turn to the development of another crucial group of potential outsider-insiders: new employees.

Table 5.1. Two Contrasting Support Infrastructures to Prepare Insiders to Wear Two Hats

	BigFab	HiTech
Culture	• Hierarchical • Authorization • Risk averse	• Lateral networks • Meritocracy • Disciplined change
Identifying potential outsider-insiders	• A rigorous nomination and selection process that begins with a manager identifying a potential candidate. • The pool of candidates is reviewed by a high-level operations committee, and then the top candidates are interviewed by four to five senior vice presidents.	• Although managers often suggest candidates, many self-nominate themselves. • Potential candidates must write an essay and then argue persuasively in a ten-minute presentation to senior executives as to why HiTech should invest in their development. • Potential candidates compete solely on their merits.
Maintaining linkages	• Initially, insiders on the outside had a mentor or person to keep in touch with them and assist them upon return. • After a few years, an active support network of managers who previously went through the full immersion process began quarterly teleconferences that include current insiders who are on the outside.	• Linkages are left up to the individual. • Many keep in touch with members of their network through periodic e-mails or telephone calls.
Clarifying reentry expectations	• Senior executive involvement in the selection process sends a clear message that it is important to both engineering and operations that these new outsider-insiders have a mission to enhance the competency base and better integrate the two functions.	• It is clear from one's first day of employment at HiTech that one's development activities and how one's ideas or perspectives will be used are mostly driven by individual initiative.
Returning home	• Initial jobs on return from school are designed to build credibility for engineers in manufacturing. • Senior-level mentors or coaches serve as a vaccine to fight the organizational immune system.	• Personal networks play a major role with a little help from informal mentors. • Because of the meritocracy, returning employees are protected from a peer performance ranking process for a year to give them time to reestablish themselves.

Chapter Six

Preparing Outsiders to Wear Two Hats

The second avenue for organizations striving to create a critical mass of outsider-insiders is to bring in outsiders and encourage them to continually address challenges with fresh perspectives, the way they do during their first few months on the job, whether that's done systematically or not. In other words, teach outsiders how to wear two hats. This is no small feat. All too often, new employees get quickly integrated into the existing culture and lose their outsider perspectives. Since newcomers want to be accepted by others in their new organization, many attempt to conform to existing norms and avoid questioning existing ways of doing things. At the other extreme are those recruits who believe in the pushcart notion of change and take the opportunity of being an outsider to throw out trial balloons filled with new ideas. Without care, they generate so many waves that it inhibits their ability to be accepted and destroys any chance for building credibility for their outsider concepts. When the latter occurs, potential outsider-insiders begin questioning whether they made a wise employment choice. Many of those who decide to stay find the path of least resistance to be conformity to existing norms and expectations: they become insiders. Organizations must therefore find ways to protect and nurture outsider perspectives while helping outsiders to develop the second half of the equation: becoming a valued and respected insider.

Since newcomers have not participated in prior decisions or actions that may have precipitated existing challenges, they do not have personal ownership in whatever problems they see. This makes it easier for them to quickly perceive gaps between observed practice and the potential root causes of problems that many insiders miss. But they often have difficulty finding the right levers to help their new organizations pull in changes that help overcome the challenges. Although they are now outsiders physically on the inside, they have yet to earn insider status. To become outsider-insiders, they must dig beneath the surface to appreciate the cultural assumptions underlying practices they observe and build support for alternative approaches to solving the challenges, that is, build credibility for themselves and their ideas.

Technically, outsiders run the gamut from people totally outside the enterprise to employees who may be internal to the organization but an outsider to a particular group, function, or site. As we saw in the previous chapter, outsiders from other functions or locations can indeed become outsider-insiders within their new group. Although many of the issues we will explore in this chapter apply to all outsiders, people who are totally green to an organization typically have a more difficult transition and are therefore the focus of this chapter. Since they have no predisposed notion of what is or is not accepted internally, they can really "push the envelope" with their outsider perspectives. But because they do not understand the existing culture, they can easily misread signals and situations.

Many new recruits have little to no work experience. These entry-level recruits may eventually develop into outsider-insiders, but they face a steep learning curve in understanding organizational life. They bring very fresh perspectives but may be so green that their ideas have little relevance to existing challenges. They may see problems but are unable to link them to the root cause of issues facing the organization; they may not even have the organizational language to express what they see. And because such "newbies" are moldable, they may be too easily assimilated into being insiders who are unable to question the system. Of course, we also find eager beavers who want to quickly show their value by trying to introduce new ideas but end up alienating themselves from the rest of the organization because they are oblivious to the importance of leveraging the existing culture.

Experienced outsiders have the best chance of quickly becoming outsider-insiders. Presumably they have already learned how to avoid many of the common mistakes of entry-level employees. As former insiders, they understand that levers are needed for successful introduction of new ideas, and as recent outsiders, they can more readily see the gaps that insiders tend to overlook. Since they have worked in other firms, they have already lived with organizational politics. Ideally, they were outsider-insiders in their prior organizations and already know how to wear two hats. They now have to learn the cultural assumptions in their new organization, but they have an experience base to build on to expedite the credibility-building process.

Unfortunately, even experienced recruits and their organizations find the entry process to be a very rocky road. Although they are hired in part to bring in their experience and knowledge, many complain that their new organizations do not value their prior experiences. Granted, the champions who hired them most likely value their skills and perspectives, but many traditional insiders may not be as supportive and complain about the baggage new recruits bring with them. But it is exactly this baggage—the outsider perspectives—that is of value, provided the newcomer properly uses it and is supported along the way.

In many respects, the situation for newcomers to an organization is analogous to the challenges facing outsider-insiders when they return from full immersion on the outside: they need a support infrastructure similar to the one we saw in Chapter Five. Here the focus is twofold: (1) quickly plunging new recruits into the culture without stifling their outsider perspectives and (2) jump-starting the credibility-building process to help new recruits become insiders without negating the value of their outsider perspectives. Before exploring the components of an effective infrastructure, we first look at why such systems are necessary to help newly recruited outsiders learn to wear two hats. The following case illustrates how a group of well-intentioned executives got blindsided by a deeply embedded culture that played itself out in unintended ways when they attempted to bring in new talent to address a critical organizational challenge.

What Can Go Wrong

Electronics Manufacturing Corporation was facing severe international competition and losing market share to global manufacturers. As senior executives attempted to introduce a number of new initiatives to ease the problem, they recognized they needed to attract a new cadre of engineers who understood manufacturing and had a passion to upgrade manufacturing competencies within their factories—a macro challenge similar to that of several other companies mentioned before. As with Rustbelt, the executives decided to recruit new blood with the hope of developing these new people into outsider-insiders who could help introduce alternative approaches within manufacturing. One manager explained their strategy: "We were afraid of losing it all. We did a number of things to counter the global threat. . . . We needed to get the best and the brightest into manufacturing. We had to understand how to win their hearts and minds. We wanted to get them to come in and to figure out how to change things."

In the end, Electronics was successful in attracting a number of potential outsider-insiders. Although a number of them developed into successful leaders, the vast majority of these recruits ended up leaving the organization within two to five years. In many respects, the executives and many of the recruits didn't understand the concept of finding micro-level challenges that would help to pull in alternative approaches at the workplace. They just assumed that the mere presence of these newcomers would drive change. But their story also highlights the importance of creating a support infrastructure for the new talent. As one of the recruits recalled, "I think they wanted to sprinkle us around the organization and hoped the flowers would grow and sprout up without a strategy of how to do it. They just threw the seeds out to fall wherever they did. . . . We were just viewed as very smart people that they wanted to let grow and do their thing."

The story began when a group of champions at the level of vice president made promises to the potential outsider-insiders to get them to join Electronics. The talent the executives targeted was in high demand since they were a rare commodity: engineers who understood the entire enterprise, both the business and technical sides, and wanted to work in manufacturing. However, these recruits did not want to wait the normal ten to twenty years that it took to get to leadership roles in Electronics' experience-based manufacturing culture. They also wanted to move across functions—manufacturing and product development, plus marketing and finance—to gain a broad-based experience, something unheard of in this siloed organization. They therefore demanded, and received promises for, accelerated cross-functional career paths, mentors, and high salaries. Unfortunately, delivery on those promises was ultimately the responsibility of local managers, not the executives who had made the commitments. The resources, such as budgets, to support the new recruits resided at the factory level.

Furthermore, little was done to prepare the organization for the new recruits, especially within the factories where they were assigned. From the executives' perspective, they identified a problem and recognized the need to pull in new people with fresh ideas to help solve their situation. They assumed these new people were so talented that others would immediately see their value. But most members of the organization, particularly the new recruits' immediate supervisors, felt these new people were being pushed on them. They viewed the newcomers as corporate-anointed fast-trackers receiving preferential treatment, something that the local managers just had to live with. As one factory manager recalled, "There was absolutely no commitment at the plant at all. In fact as managers, we were punished. They [the new recruits] were being paid exorbitant salaries out of our budgets. . . . Someone high up decided to hire them and a few levels below saw that and each took one, saying 'I'm in.'"

The combination of cross-functional rotational assignments and fast-track careers ran counter to cultural assumptions around the criteria for adding value to the organization. Local managers viewed tenure on the job as the number-one criterion for building credibility. As a result, the newcomers were quickly labeled "high maintenance," by which they meant more trouble than they were worth for their immediate supervisors, who viewed them as trainees en route to bigger opportunities. Furthermore, the supervisors, already swamped with their normal daily demands, felt overburdened by having to manage newcomers who didn't understand the organization and made it clear that they didn't want to stay around long enough to learn. An outsider-insider who was able to rise above the stigma described the situation:

> At a prior company, I told my manager I wanted to rotate around. The defining moment of my career was when he told me, "You are worse than zero value because you are drawing a salary." For the first seven months, I saw my job as an internal consultant. The problem was that the organization had no way of knowing what I was and they had no way of knowing how to interact with me. From that point on, I started working on projects, and I have been seen as hugely successful.

But the other new recruits did not have the benefit of such coaching. Most expected rotational assignments of relatively short duration. After all, their generation was being told that they should expect eight to ten career changes during their working life, and many members of their peer group in less experienced-based organizations were jumping from one job to another to broaden their résumés. But local managers lived by Electronics' norms and began dragging their feet on moving the developing outsider-insiders to new assignments; they wanted some payback for supporting the effort. When this occurred, the new recruits perceived a rift between promises that were made to them and the reality of factory life within Electronics. After all, as one manager noted, "The new recruits came in assuming what they were told in the recruiting process would be true."

When the newcomers encountered the difference between promise and reality, some left the company, while others went back to the executives who hired them. Both routes fueled the local suspicion that these people were high-maintenance folks. The champions, however, had invested personal time and energy in recruiting these individuals; they did not want to lose them. So the executives helped the newcomers find other opportunities, often in another factory. But the cycle just repeated itself in the new assignments. Before long, many remaining developing outsider-insiders concluded that they could do better elsewhere and resigned from the company. As one manager recalled, rather than the newcomers helping to transform the culture, the culture expelled the newcomers: "It didn't just create some consternation; they got spit out. It didn't work at all. . . . They were put into a pool of sharks. I guess they assumed that their experience would make them a shark and they would survive, but the true sharks ate them alive."

Alas, this is not an extreme case by any means. Few organizational cultures are friendly to outsider perspectives, especially those coming from people who have not yet established credibility as insiders. Without a clear plan and process, potential outsider-insiders often become frustrated and leave before they have a chance to use their outsider perspectives to help address organizational challenges. A manager at another company noted, "Since we don't have clear plans about why we want them beside the fact that they are good resources, we don't recruit carefully enough to find the right fit so that once they are hired, they aren't disappointed and leave."

In retrospect, it is fairly easy to see how Electronics got itself into the "doom cycle" mapped out in Figure 6.1. It all began when the executives made promises to the outsiders without first aligning the rest of the organization. The local managers did not feel empowered to say no to their corporate leaders and therefore went through the motions to accommodate the new recruits. But there was such a cultural divide between the expectations of the newcomers and the insiders within Electronics that the system just "spit out" the developing outsider-insiders. The result was frustration on the part of all stakeholders: the executive champions, the local managers and supervisors, and the developing outsider-insiders.

Figure 6.1. The Doom Cycle

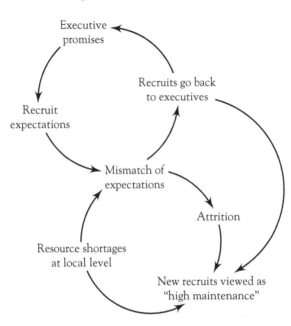

Worse yet, the outsiders became high-maintenance recruits rather than outsider-insiders who could wear their two hats to help the organization address its key challenges. Granted, the newcomers could easily see the low-hanging fruit, but they never got a chance to become insiders and work within the culture to find opportunities to pull in their outsider perspectives.

Building a Support Infrastructure to Jump-Start the Outsider-Insider Development Journey

Happily, there is an alternative to the doom cycle. It requires an organizational strategy and an infrastructure parallel to the one we saw in Chapter Five. As with insiders learning to wear two hats, this infrastructure begins before individuals are selected for development—in this case, before the hiring decision itself. As we saw in Chapter Three, there needs to be an alignment of all stakeholders around a macro challenge. Then, and only then, is the organization ready to begin identifying potential outsiders to bring in and develop into outsider-insiders. Once the outsiders are inside the organization, they then need help to quickly learn the culture and build credibility as insiders. And along the way, all parties need to be periodically reminded that it is important for the organization to value outsider-insider perspectives.

Left to their own accord, new employees will eventually learn their way around, but organizations can do many things to help jump-start the process that keeps them from being totally assimilated. In contrast to the Electronics case where one bad move led to another, it is possible to create an infrastructure that successfully develops outsiders into a cadre of outsider-insiders. In contrast to ending up with anomalies parachuted in to make changes, the cycle outlined in Figure 6.2 leads to building a critical mass of recruits who can join newly developed outsider-insiders from within to begin finding opportunities to pull in alternative approaches to address macro challenges. Hence, it is important to integrate the infrastructure of new recruits with parallel development efforts for insiders (the infrastructure outlined in Chapter Five). The amalgamation of the two infrastructures helps to minimize any hard feelings on the part of insiders that outsiders are being given preferential treatment, as was the case at Electronics. And as we saw with the journey for insiders learning to question their assumptions, the successful transition from being outsiders to outsider-insiders is a joint effort between the outsiders learning to wear two hats and their organizations. All this is critical for building the capability for true change.

In the following pages, we will explore each part of the "outsider to outsider-insider" infrastructure (the shaded box in Figure 6.2) and show how the execution of each element must fit with the existing culture rather than fight it. BigFab and HiTech once again serve as our comparative best practice cases. As we have already

Figure 6.2. Infrastructure for Preparing Outsiders to Wear Two Hats

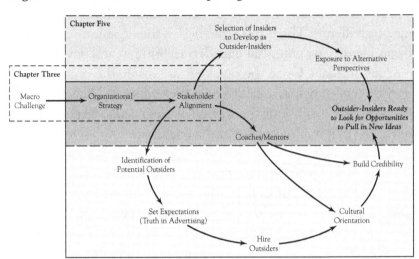

detailed, both companies had a macro challenge—increasing cost competitiveness at BigFab and a capacity shortfall at HiTech—and recognized the need to create a critical mass of outsider-insiders to help address them. As would be expected, their two infrastructures for preparing outsiders to wear two hats are quite different: BigFab relies on a formal sponsor-driven approach where senior executives provide mentoring and protection for new recruits. HiTech's infrastructure is less structured, with individuals taking the lead role in managing their own development process. But in both cases, a key to their success is a careful screening of potential recruits to make sure they will fit in and be comfortable working within their respective cultures.

Attracting the Right Outsiders

Attracting the right outsiders (that is, those who will be able to develop into effective, proactive outsider-insiders) is difficult, especially for organizations that tend to be insular. Although these are the companies that most need such outsiders, attracting them is often a hard sell. Potential outsider-insiders are not the typical newly hired employee. Finding outsiders who can wear two hats is different from merely finding a specific skill set or filling an existing job opening. Essentially, organizations are looking for "two-fers": individuals who possess both specific knowledge and expertise needed to respond to a macro challenge or to fill a competency shortfall, plus the potential to build credibility as an insider while retaining their ability to question their own and their organization's assumptions. Furthermore, potential outsider-insiders must buy into the organization's strategic directions and basic values.

Organizations often blame recruiting processes for their lack of success in attracting these people, but it is rarely just the recruiters who are at fault. It is a lack of an infrastructure to support the right people once they enter the firm. As one outsider-insider noted, "We look at pieces, like recruiting, rather than the entire system and ask why people are not coming to our company." Potential outsider-insiders, like the ones at Electronics, are not only looking at the entry job assignment and compensation; they want to know whether they will be in a position to use their outsider perspectives to find opportunities to pull in change. This requires help in navigating the foreign, and potentially hostile, culture they are entering and influential champions to occasionally run interference for them. So even if senior leadership, like the ones at Electronics, recognize that they need to build a critical mass of outsider-insiders at the working level, the culture, especially if it is risk averse and experience based, discourages top talent from even considering the company. One outsider-insider who was trying to help senior executives in the recruiting effort at such a company noted, "The company was kidding themselves if they thought that they could go and just say when they offer someone a job, 'Trust us. We will take care of you.'"

Initially, BigFab had a similar problem. Because it was an experience-based culture, working one's way up from the bottom was the expected starting point for all new employees. Similar experience on the outside, such as having been a first-line supervisor in another organization, was not valued. This made BigFab unattractive to experienced prospective outsiders, who feared it would be difficult to break into the culture and create the needed sponsorship of influential leaders to build credibility for their outsider perspectives. As one of BigFab's outsider-insiders recalled, "Our company is older with lots of old management. It takes a long time to become a vice president in a place like this. There are no forty-year-old VPs here. So you have to work your way up from the bottom, and that puts people off. Also the jobs they offer to outsiders are just *not* appealing. . . . Until BigFab understands a career path, they won't hire outsiders."

Although BigFab had a tradition of identifying and nurturing internal high-potential talent—that is, influential sponsors watched over specific individuals and provided key career opportunities so they could take a fast-track through the organization—little thought had been given to bringing in experienced outsiders. The organization just assumed that outsiders would start at the bottom and work their way up the hierarchy. But as BigFab started to hire experienced professionals, it discovered it needed a similar infrastructure for outsiders learning to wear two hats. Senior executives became directly involved in the recruiting process to show outsiders that they would be valued on an equal par with internal outsider-insiders in the company's authorization culture. Furthermore, BigFab turned to its newly developed outsider-insiders from within to help illustrate that it was possible to learn to wear and use two hats within this risk-averse organization. They became role models for prospective recruits and coaches for those who were hired.

A key difference between BigFab and Electronics was recognition of the need to work with the culture as opposed to going against it. BigFab leveraged its hierarchical environment by having senior executives personally involved in the development of newcomers whom they hoped would learn to wear two hats. This was not something left to local managers as it was at Electronics. The executive mentors provided the authorization for bringing in the developing outsiders to introduce new ideas. They also sent a message to the entire organization that these were the types of perspectives they personally valued, a big recruiting tool for attracting potential outsider-insiders.

In contrast to BigFab, HiTech was in the enviable position of being a very attractive company for potential outsider-insiders due to its high growth. Its problem was screening rather than attracting outside applicants. Many outsiders wanted to work at HiTech, but only a fraction understood or would be comfortable working within its disciplined change culture. As a result, HiTech relied heavily on the use of behavioral interviews, in which they asked candidates how they might address key situations, to identify whether a candidate's prior attempts at introducing new ideas would fit within their environment. As one recently recruited outsider noted,

> They do behavioral interviews and deselect people who don't fit. The interview process is that they first identify the skill sets needed for the job, and they break it into categories—technical and behavioral. Then they ask questions about whether you have done this before and how did you handle it. For example, they try to figure out whether a person is comfortable in a changing, dynamic situation. They asked, "What did you do if you had multiple meetings booked in the same time slot?" or "What did you do when your boss gave you conflicting priorities?"

The behavioral interviews served two purposes: to identify the right outsiders and to begin setting expectations around what it would be like at HiTech, another piece of the infrastructure for preparing outsiders to wear two hats.

Truth in Advertising

Recruiting processes, even those relying on behavioral interviews, typically resemble marketing propaganda for both recruiters and candidates. Both parties attempt to convince each other that they have what it takes for a perfect fit. But as we saw with Electronics, this often ends in unfilled promises and misaligned expectations on what the new employee will experience and what the organization can deliver. Electronics' corporate management made promises based on where it hoped to move the organization rather than on the current state of the culture, a common error when organizations are attempting to hire talent with critical skills that are in short supply. The painful lesson is that organizations need a careful screening process that heavily weighs a candidate's fit with the culture coupled to an up-front, honest description of what the company really values.

With today's emphasis on workforce diversity, there is often a reluctance to raise the issue of cultural fit. As one manager in a company that prided itself on its inclusivity noted, "It would be politically incorrect to ask about cultural fit." But honesty about the existing culture is critical. Many outsiders are hired to help transform organizations, yet its current state is glossed over because there is a fear that revealing how archaic prospective organizations really are might dissuade potential recruits.

Truth in advertising is similar to setting expectations for development activities for insiders, but gaining clarity with outsiders is often more difficult since a common language needs to be created. Using organizational shorthand with outsiders leaves potential recruits to interpret promises using their outsider assumptions, which may or may not match internal notions of what role outsiders are in fact to play. One particular area for a likely mismatch is the speed with which outsider ideas are likely to be implemented. As we have seen, the road to credibility as an insider in experience-based organizations is primarily time, and lots of it. But the amount of time and the breadth of influence a developing outsider-insider might have are typically glossed over during the recruiting process. One manager in an extremely risk-averse organization put it this way, "After the first two assignments, they should have learned the ropes, and then they can make a lot of local changes. They can influence what is done in their area—at that point they have enough credibility, confidence, and knowledge."

Such clarity, however, emerged only after many newcomers in this organization grew deeply frustrated. As one new recruit who left after one year with the company stated, "There is learning and then there is a feeling of self-fulfillment and having an impact quickly. . . . They want me to learn the system first before I can do some things like lead and change things. My view is that you lead and change while learning."

This mismatch of expectations could and should have been avoided. If there had been more truth in advertising during the recruiting process, on both the individual's and the organization's part, this person would most likely have chosen to go elsewhere. He would have saved himself a year of frustration and saved the company the cost of recruiting and developing him.

For BigFab and HiTech, truth in advertising was generally not an issue. Their cultures are so pervasive that all recruits had to do was walk through the halls during interview visits to feel it. "There is a culture here that is clear and specific," one HiTech insider pointed out. "I'm not sure if it is done by hiring or brainwashing or whether you just absorb it from being here."

But even with the culture's intensity, recruiters, as we saw, were still screened for fit by using behavior interviews to make sure candidates clearly understood what it would be like to work in HiTech's disciplined change culture. Such a recruiting strategy is not as simple when an organization lacks a unified culture. This is particularly true in highly decentralized firms or those that recently have gone through an acquisition or merger. Unfortunately, recruiters often assume that candidates will eventually find a good fit somewhere. This assumption tends to backfire, especially if the potential outsider-insiders are looking for cross-functional or cross-divisional development assignments that land them in a culture that is not fitted to their personal skill set. It would be like moving someone between HiTech and BigFab. Some outsider-insiders might view it as an opportunity to hone their outsider perspectives, but others would likely fall flat on their face.

Most important, however, is that truth in advertising helps to ease the transition from the outside to the inside. The wining and dining associated with many recruiting processes often leads to unrealistic expectations that special treatment will continue after hiring, which rarely happens. Said one manager:

> Any special treatment stops the minute you get in the door. People get lavish attention during recruiting and then they are not even greeted at the front door on their first day at work. It's not as nurturing as you might be led to expect. . . . We throw you out there with the other fish and see how you do. That's the way it is for everybody. It's our egalitarian way of doing things. You just come in and prove yourself. That may not always be the best but that's how we do it.

Recruiting processes must be honest about both insider and outsider expectations after hiring. But attracting and getting the right outsiders in the door is only the beginning. The newcomers must now become assimilated without being "culturalized," a difficult balancing act for new recruits, who must retain outsider perspectives while learning the organizational culture and building credibility as an insider. From an organizational perspective, this means providing room for them to retain outsider perspectives—in other words, developing an organizational acceptance of outsider perspectives and an environment that nourishes outsider-insiders and builds a bridge between the outside and inside worlds. Once the bridge is built, it is an easy trip to move from one side to the other, that is, to wear two hats. But the bridge needs a strong foundation and grows stronger with each support beam that gets added. And just as new concrete needs to set and strengthen, creating a supportive environment takes time and patience on the part of both developing outsider-insiders and other organizational members.

Getting to Know the Existing Culture

As we saw in Chapter Four, the existing culture is one of an outsider-insider's key levers in helping others to see where underlying assumptions are getting in the way of overcoming challenges. Hence, one of the first things new employees need to do is learn the whys and wherefores of the existing culture. As we saw with insiders on development assignments on the outside, such learning emerges from total immersion into the workplace to see the culture in action. BigFab recognized this and gave its new recruits some time and space to explore their new home. A BigFab executive noted, "We need to give them some grounding and do some stage setting. When Lester came here, we told him to spend thirty days just wandering around and learning the ropes before he got into the fray."

This approach is in stark contrast to what happens in many organizations, especially entrepreneurial ones, which tend to leave the learning and exploration up to the new recruits without the benefit of grounding and stage setting and then gauge their ability to fit in as a measure of their interpersonal skills. Certainly any newcomer must be attuned to and willing to adjust to cultural nuances, but there are many things an organization can, and should, do to jump-start the process.

HiTech, for example, doesn't leave anything to chance; there is no "wandering around" here, including learning about its ubiquitous culture. The company is deeply involved in providing ongoing formal training and coaching in HiTech ways of doing things, beginning with a one-week orientation on the HiTech culture. But learning the espoused values and explicitly stated desired behavior is only the first step at any company, not just HiTech. As most newcomers quickly learn, every company has organizational ambiguities that take time to decode. These cultural nuances exist in even the most rational, data-driven firms. A HiTech manager observed, "There can be conflicting messages. You need to hear the message in the context of what is going on in the environment. You need to have a history and understand the environment. The issue is how to jump-start the history."

Formal classroom training needs to be supplemented with on-the-job coaching to aid the learning process. As with insiders learning to wear two hats, outsiders need "tour guides" to help them decipher the nuances to truly understand the underlying assumptions behind the behavior they observe.

In BigFab, new recruits are matched to a senior-level adviser who helps them translate what they are experiencing and break through hierarchical issues they encounter. In HiTech's meritocratic culture, in contrast, mentors and coaches are informal or short term, in the form of voluntary coaches; for example, there is a voluntary Web-based buddy system whereby new recruits can link up with a coach or adviser for a few months. Individuals who are interested in providing guidance to others or are looking for coaches can identify themselves. Potential advisers are then matched to those desiring coaches based on competencies, skills, and goals of both parties. The expectation is that both will commit to one to four hours of interaction per month for a length of time agreed to between them. Typically, the initial agreement is to meet for four to six months. After that, developing outsider-insiders are expected to build their own network of coaches and mentors, another reflection of the meritocratic culture.

In addition to being cultural tour guides, coaches or mentors can help newcomers explore ways to build credibility, the final step in learning to wear two hats. Experience shows that there are commonsense approaches, regardless of the culture, that put new recruits on a launchpad for becoming successful outsider-insiders who get their organizations behind their outsider ideas rather than resisting them. Not surprisingly, it combines learning the culture with building a base of support. One manager described the style of an entering outsider: "He wins people over. . . . He's very non-threatening. . . . He didn't come in with all the answers. . . . His approach was to get to know people, understand their point of view, communicate in the language they understand, and establish alliances with the workforce."

Building Credibility

While organizations can help with the cultural learning process through training and coaching, newly recruited outsiders must own the lion's share of credibility building. When a newcomer is closely associated with a highly regarded insider, there may be some initial referent credibility, a bit of a halo effect that at least puts the outsider on a good footing.[1] But whether that status lasts past the first handshake is really up to the entering outsider. This is as true in an entrepreneurial organization as it is in a risk-averse one.

Building credibility comprises two parts: displaying competence and showing relevance of outsider perspectives. The first part involves demonstrating that developing outsider-insiders understand the cultural underpinnings of the organization; the second requires using outsider concepts to deliver results and meet performance objectives. Both take time to build and are continually tested. "You have to walk before you run, and you have to run before you fly," commented one manager. "Otherwise, you will not have the respect of the people you will be working with." Organizations and their newly recruited outsiders must be patient; the process of building credibility as an insider does not occur overnight. As another manager observed, "During the first couple of years, new recruits are just learning the company. There is a two-year point where their perspective changes. They have paid their dues, they have figured the company out, they have built their mentors and relationships, and they have their networks."

There is nothing magical about the two-year time period this manager cited. Some outsiders are quick studies, and their personal values and style are so attuned to working in the existing culture that they become outsider-insiders in a few months. For example, HiTech provides a one-year moratorium from its peer ranking to learn the culture and build credibility. After all, the organization carefully selects outsiders who will naturally fit in the culture. But others need more assistance either because of their maturity or the cultural barriers they face. In all cases, however, the newly recruited outsiders must recognize the need and be willing to learn about the existing culture they are entering rather than just pushing their ideas onto others, an expectation that should have been set during truth in advertising. As one of BigFab's managers said:

They need time to build relationships and a network. I had a coun-
seling session with one recruit prior to him accepting our offer. The
BigFab [developing outsider-insiders from within] know what to
expect when they come back [from full-immersion assignments on
the outside], but new hires don't understand about the culture here.
Change doesn't happen quickly. It takes a long time. Many get
frustrated because it is not happening quickly enough. They all
have the skills to succeed. But they have to have the right personality; they have to be able to meld into the environment. BigFab
has a real old-school management.

Building credibility in experience-based companies like BigFab
typically means working one's way up from the bottom, even if that
means repeating assignments held in other companies. As in many
other manufacturing organizations, the first true test of survival is a
stint as a first-line supervisor. One of BigFab's executive outsider-
insiders who came in from the outside after being a manager at
another large organization recalled being aware that "I had to first
develop face credibility. I was willing to be a first-line manager
without feeling like I was losing status or esteem." The supervisory
assignment is considered a rite of passage for newly recruited
outsiders—the way they prove their mettle in the manufacturing
organization. An outsider-insider at another equally risk-averse
company referred to supervisory experience as "a litmus test" not-
ing, "In manufacturing, it gives you organizational credibility."

Building credibility also means learning to play by the rules, that
is, conform to norms of behavior, at least until one is accepted as an
insider. This was a lesson learned the hard way for Sam, one of
BigFab's first outsiders hired. Sam eventually became a successful
outsider-insider progressing up the hierarchical ladder to become an
executive, but the road was rocky and, in many respects, an individual companion story to the Electronics doom cycle. His experience
highlighted the need for BigFab to develop an "outsider to outsider-
insider" infrastructure. In fact, his story became legend internally as
an exemplar of what not to do as a newly recruited outsider.

Sam had previously worked at an entrepreneurial company and started as a college intern working on a project that convinced executives that they could save $120 million in inventory costs by rearranging the assembly operation. He assumed that his ideas would be equally welcome on the shop floor, but when he got there, he learned otherwise. As one of his early managers recalled,

> He [Sam] had lots of ideas but he had to learn that he was not God's gift to the factory. He did not get along with the shop floor manager and we were close to having a standstill—a real crisis—on the line. And we could not have that. It took us less than thirty days to move him out of here. He just didn't fit in with the culture. . . . It was the wrong time and the wrong ideas. He is brilliant—he's got the creativity, he thinks things through analytically. But it is part of the culture—to have right-minded ideas, but with good timing.

The culture "spit him out," at least initially. Sam did not start off listening and learning from insiders. He "came in with all the answers," the exact opposite of the universal approach to gaining acceptance internally. In BigFab's experience-based culture, veterans had the upper hand. As another BigFab manager noted, "Sam had some problems in the beginning. He wanted to change things with a guy who had been here for thirty-five years. And he talked a lot of high-falutin' technical crap. So the people on the shop floor had not much choice but to back the veteran."

Fortunately, Sam recovered from his early missteps. As he quickly recognized, building credibility for outsider ideas in a culture like BigFab requires listening and learning before trying to introduce alternative ways of doing things: "I went in and made some early mistakes. In my next job, I paid attention and listened to people. I told them that they had to tell me what their problems were. I needed to get them to own the issues."

Sam's eventual success as an outsider-insider at BigFab happened only because he was willing to learn from his mistakes and setbacks. In retrospect, we can see that he could have avoided many of his problems had he followed a lower-key approach upon entry. As one of his managers summarized, "Sam learned that in order to make change, you have to build up a base and gain a position of strength." But his experience helped outsiders who followed him: he became an emblem of triumph over adversity. Furthermore, outsiders now have an infrastructure to help them learn to wear two hats, in part a result of Sam's ordeal.

As we have seen, it is possible to avoid Electronics' doom cycle, but it takes a conscious effort to develop and manage an integrated infrastructure to support outsiders through their development journey to become outsider-insiders. It also takes a concerted effort on the part of the new recruit: this is a shared process. Table 6.1 provides a summary of the various elements needed and how BigFab and HiTech have tailored the execution of the fundamentals to fit their respective cultures. We end this chapter with one more case—this one a success story of an outsider who made the ultimate transition from an old-school, risk-averse organization to a free-wheeling, entrepreneurial company.

Moving from Outsider to Outsider-Insider Status

Tony was a seasoned finance professional with a successful track record in traditional, bureaucratic organizations. His skills were severely needed by an entrepreneurial company that had experienced rapid growth but had recently hit a dramatic decline in sales. The market was also questioning the company's ability to survive over the long haul; the value of its stock price dropped from $90 to $60 in a single day. The CEO realized he needed a veteran CFO to help turn the company around, a macro challenge if there ever was one.

Tony had never worked in an entrepreneurial organization and was, not surprisingly, viewed as a total stranger to the culture. In this case, however, his outsider status was actually an advantage since everyone recognized the critical business needs for the expertise he possessed. In a technocratic organization like Tony's new company, credentials are often valued more highly than internal

Table 6.1. Two Contrasting Support Infrastructures to Prepare Outsiders to Wear Two Hats

	BigFab	HiTech
Culture	• Hierarchical • Authorization • Risk averse	• Lateral networks • Meritocracy • Disciplined change
Recruiting strategy	• Newcomers protected and placed in key assignments linked to macro pulls with managed career paths	• Scattered across the organization with future movement initiated by individual
Selection	• Interviewed by senior executives and network of outsider-insiders	• Behavioral interviews to ensure "cultural fit"
Truth in advertising	• Clarity around organizational culture • Articulated career progression	• Clear from one's first day of employment that one's development activities and how one's ideas or perspectives will be used is mostly driven by individual initiative
Learning the culture	• Mentored by senior leadership • Active network of outsider-insiders	• Intensive training around culture and internal processes • Voluntary Web-based mentor or buddy system
Building credibility	• Direct line assignments within firm	• One-year protection from peer ranking to build credibility and learn organization

knowledge or fitting in. So while everyone, including the CEO, dressed casually, Tony showed up every day in a suit and tie. But he worked in the company's "bull pen" rather than a corner office as he was accustomed to at his former employer. Over time, his tie became a symbol for his outside expertise. Such an overt display would probably never have worked in a more experience-based firm, but what mattered in this entrepreneurial organization was Tony's outside experience, provided he could deliver performance. To that end, he stood up at his first quarterly meeting and explained why he had made such a drastic career move to join a failing organization and help turn it around. He then proceeded to lay out a plan to take the stock price to $200 within two years, a promise that turned into a vision and reality.

In many respects, Tony was lucky. He entered an organization that clearly had a macro challenge that everyone recognized. He was able to quickly articulate the gap between what had been done in the past and the root cause of the current problem. He could also easily show where his outside expertise could be useful to the organization; after all, that's what he was hired to do. But beyond that, Tony was clever in how he leveraged the culture. Although he chose to use his dress as a bridge between the outside and the inside, he did conform to other internal norms, such as not having a walled office and willingly sitting out in the central bull pen. He recognized that he needed to accept certain cultural norms while using others to send a message that he wore two hats (and a tie!).

Tony was also fortunate to be brought into a senior leadership role where he could immediately use his position to find opportunities to pull in his outsider perspectives. Most outsider-insiders are not in such positions and must find ways to get to the right place at the right time in order to use their outsider perspectives to help solve micro-level challenges, the subject we turn to next.

Chapter Seven

Getting to the Right Place at the Right Time to Pull Change

Given the sheer numbers of problems lying around organizations, outsider-insiders need more than luck to ensure that they can put their ideas and skills to work on the most critical gaps. Few are as fortunate as Tony to be placed in a position recognized as needing an outsider's perspective. Many outsider-insiders, especially those who reside in the lower echelons of large hierarchies, need assistance in finding their way through their organizations' mazes. Likewise, managers who face key challenges at both the macro and micro levels need assistance in locating outsider-insiders who have appropriate competencies to help address their challenges. Both need matchmakers: scouts or friends throughout their organizations who can identify and connect outsider-insiders to key problem areas. Developing a critical mass of outsider-insiders is only the first step toward building an army of employees to create the "pong" required to address macro challenges. The final step is getting these outsider-insiders to the right place at the right time so they can apply their two-hat perspectives to finding the right opportunities to pull in new ideas and ways of doing things.

The process of matchmaking is far from obvious. Matches generally occur when someone introduces an outsider-insider to a manager who is facing a challenge that could use outsider perspectives. In many respects, it is like a dating game. Sometimes outsider-insiders who are in search of new and interesting challenges initiate the matchmaking. At other times, it is the manager facing the challenge, on the lookout for someone with the right set of skills to help overcome it. Occasionally the individual and the challenge will meet by happenstance, but more often, it is the friends of each party that make the match. These friends constitute each party's network.

Networks are a way of life within and outside organizations. Networks begin to be created well before individuals learn to wear two hats; they begin to grow from the day employees join a firm and expand as they interact with others within their new organization, one of the reasons that newcomers at BigFab were encouraged to wander around and meet people. There are also networks that bridge the inside and outside worlds, such as industry forums and university alumni groups. These networks are a formal part of the outsider-insider support infrastructure (see Figure 1.2) and must be managed. New products or ideas that are shared through networks activate hundreds of auxiliary networks. This ultimately creates a tipping point where new concepts spread like wildfire.[1] Career counselors typically tell job seekers to tap into their networks. This chapter brings together these two common uses of networks to complete the pulling change process: helping outsider-insiders to be in a position to identify gaps to pull in change.

Matchmakers come in many different forms and play a variety of roles. Some are formal mentors or sponsors of individual outsider-insiders, while others are just acquaintances who happen to know someone who might fit an organizational need. The common denominator is that they are all people who use their personal networks to help find appropriate matches. Many organizations use the terms *mentors* and *sponsors* interchangeably, but each serves a slightly different role.[2] Although one individual can serve both needs, most outsider-insiders develop a network of sponsors and mentors. Sponsors tend to be the most senior and influential helpers who act as advocates for individual outsider-insiders. Mentors are more like coaches or advisers who guide their protégés through the pulling change process and help them to expand their own networks. Generally, mentors tend to be more senior than their protégés, but not always. To be truly effective in their roles, however, sponsors and mentors must also be outsider-insiders themselves who understand the need to seek out alternative perspectives. If they aren't, they will be tempted to shape their protégés into their organization's standard mold. One of BigFab's outsider-insiders recalled, "I've had enlightened leaders who were willing to give me a chance. I was lucky to have the right champions. They had choices of people to put in different jobs, and they took a chance on me. Usually it was controversial and they didn't go with the prevailing wind."

Fortunately, senior-level outsider-insiders at BigFab have the power and influence to break free of the status quo. This is essential because hiring an outsider-insider in a risk-averse environment is an unnatural act for insiders. In this chapter, we take a deep dive into the world of matchmaking and how mentors and sponsors can both help and hinder the matchmaking process. As with other parts of the infrastructure, the matchmaking process is a shared responsibility: outsider-insiders and their organizations must work together to find the right opportunities to pull in new ideas. To begin our journey, we meet a self-proclaimed "network attractor," someone who has a large network and uses it to mobilize outsider-insiders to create the "pong."

A Network Navigator

Dan, an executive vice president and general manager at HiTech, is the quintessential outsider-insider. Although he has worked for HiTech for over twenty years and is deeply committed to helping make it successful, he has never really fit the mold. He is always pushing the envelope in how he manages his groups and continually steps back to take time for reflection. He recognizes that his approach is often viewed as countercultural within HiTech and that he needs a critical mass of like-minded folks to help him attain his strategic objectives. One of his managers noted, "Dan is building a network of competent people throughout the company that he can leverage. He hires people who can translate his vision into reality. . . . As he understands the problems, he pulls the right people from across the organization to solve the problems. He has the ability to identify the people with the right skill sets that fit the problem."

Dan's own outsider perspectives have been shaped by a variety of life and career experiences, including expatriate assignments in Asia and Europe. These experiences have helped him to recognize multiple points of view that enable him to break down traditional territorial boundaries. This made him a natural for overseeing the integration of a newly acquired European division—the macro challenge in this case. The division had a proud entrepreneurial history and was reluctant to buy into HiTech's disciplined change ways of doing things. Dan's task was complicated by the need to align the new division to a corporate strategy that required them to outsource some of their testing to HiTech's Asian operation.[3]

Dan could have managed the integration from afar, but he realized the importance of learning the culture of the newly acquired division from within. So he packed up his family and relocated to Europe. One of his first tasks was to identify and team up two working-level outsider-insiders—one in Asia, the other in Europe—to implement the outsourcing strategy. Since he had spent several years working in the Asian operation, it was relatively easy for him to tap into his network to find an appropriate Asian team lead. Being physically located within the new division also helped him to quickly find an outsider-insider who was aligned with his mission. This was an art he had honed to perfection:

> My role in this company is to be an air traffic controller, that is, stick to the big picture, communicate the overall context and purpose, and help people connect with other people that can assist or bring insights to the problem. Then let them free to find ways to add value. . . . We need to be very specific and cautious when selecting people, making sure they have the right skills, and even more important, that they have the right network to tap into in order to pull knowledge into the team and diffuse it out in the organization.

Although there were bumps along the road, the two team leaders quickly recognized the value each other's organization had to share, and the two became internal advocates for integration within their respective groups. Because Dan had taken care to clearly articulate the strategic importance of their mission, they had the power of the larger organization behind them. The result was a swift and successful transfer of the European division's test activities to Asia. In effect, as the Europeans and the Asians began working together as one organization, true change was the result.

Dan provided two essential ingredients for successful implementation of outsider perspectives at the local level. First, he linked the need for those outside ideas to a strategic business objective: the macro challenge (Chapter Three). The locals in both Europe and Asia may not have initially liked the idea, but at least they knew why they needed to make the test transfer work. It wasn't just the two local outsider-insiders who were pushing their perspectives onto their peers. Rather, those outsider perspectives were being brought inside to solve a key business challenge that would ultimately make the overall organization, including the two local groups, more competitive. Second, Dan was the sponsor for integrating the operations and, by inference, the sponsor for the two team leads. The two quickly trusted each other based on their allegiance to Dan. They recognized that he valued both of them and wouldn't be asking them to work together unless he knew they both could accomplish the task.[4] Furthermore, the rest of the organization recognized that Dan was the sponsor, which provided cover and clout for the two team leads. Through working on the project, the two team leads broadened their own networks, which, in turn, prepared them to be future matchmakers like Dan.

Developing Personal Networks to Get to the Right Place at the Right Time

As Dan's story illustrates, personal networks are critical conduits for matchmaking. Although sponsors and mentors often become the focal point in this process, it is their networks that in fact serve as the mechanism for pairing up individual outsider-insiders to specific micro challenges. "It is part mentoring and part networking," explained an outsider-insider. "It is just part of getting to know someone with a particular expertise. It is the way to navigate through the organization."

There are two ways that outsider-insider networks get built: informal interaction with peers and relationships created through job assignments. While the former tends to be driven by an individual's ability to build credibility for their ideas and expertise, the latter is highly dependent on the organization's support infrastructure. But as seen in Figure 7.1, each feeds the other to create a reinforcing cycle.

The right-hand loop begins when someone exchanges an idea through informal interaction with a peer, such as sharing an idea or asking for help in solving a problem. As one outsider-insider said, "Knowledge transfer happens by personal contact. It's kind of like, 'Hey, you want to talk to so and so. He knows this and that.'" Although most organizations have extensive knowledge management systems, many people first ask a friend or work associate for help before searching data repositories or contacting an expert they have never met. In other words, they use their networks to find people who hold alternative perspectives or have the expertise to help overcome the challenges they face. Even when they use formal systems, the database may send them to someone who then

Figure 7.1. Pulling Change Through Personal Networks

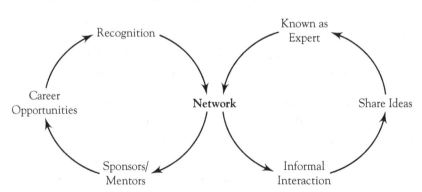

refers them to a member of his or her network who possesses the exact expertise needed to solve the challenge. That's the wonderful thing about networks: they grow exponentially. Each interaction creates a new node since every network member brings along his or her own contacts and friends. Dan, our network navigator, was well aware of the benefits of tapping into both internal and external networks. For this reason, he was an active mentor for several developing outsider-insiders who had been recently hired by HiTech. As he explained,

> A real asset is their relationships with colleagues both within HiTech and other companies. It is an outstanding network for finding expertise to solve problems. I leverage it a lot to solve problems of a systemic nature, ones that are not proprietary in nature. I can call one or two of them and within twenty-four hours have a hundred people helping me solve a problem with recommendations of places to go to see things.

Networks, like Dan's, benefit both the organization and the network members by providing a mechanism to link outsider perspectives to urgent and important challenges. When a new idea or way of approaching a problem is pulled in to solve a problem, the individual who identified an alternative approach, the outsider-insider, becomes known for his or her expertise, or access to the expertise, in solving such challenges. When a similar challenge arises, someone in the individual's network identifies the expert as the person to contact to address the challenge.

Networks also lead to and are the result of career moves: the left-hand side of Figure 7.1. Dan created an extensive network as he moved from North America to Asia and then Europe. He then used that network to help other outsider-insiders be in a position to use their two hats to help overcome organizational challenges. Similarly, individuals who move from one functional group to another create diversified networks that afford them a chance to mentor other outsider-insiders and find opportunities to diffuse outsider perspectives. As one young engineer observed, "Sharing between the divisions was initiated by one manager who had been around the circuit and knew people. There was another guy who had worked in a couple of plants who also initiated some of the sharing. It was the personnel transfers that made the linkages."

As outsider-insiders travel between organizational units and encounter challenges in their new locale, their mental models become different from those of their local peers. In other words, each career move hones outsider perspectives and further builds network links. One executive outsider-insider put it this way: "As I've moved from one job to another, I've found new ways to apply those [outsider] tools and new tools to add to my tool kit." In this way, each assignment opens the door for finding opportunities to pull change through the organization.

Every time an outsider-insider's solution solves a new challenge, more people become supporters or mentors looking out for additional challenges where the expert can apply his or her capabilities. Success in these assignments then leads to further recognition and more people added to one's network—and more matchmakers. Ultimately, one creates an extensive network that provides a platform to help match both oneself and others to key challenges as they arrive. These networks help outsider-insiders link their ideas to more macro challenges facing the organization. As one outsider-insider noted, "In a company with different divisions that are very distributed, if you don't have a network, you'll never get the information you need. If you don't have people to connect to, you can't understand what's going on. Managing things in your own four walls is easy; it's looking outside that's hard." In other words, networks become instrumental in connecting local-level pings to create the pong we talked about in Chapter Three.

Significantly, networks are equally important in both risk-averse and entrepreneurial cultures. The only difference is that the influential networks in entrepreneurial firms tend to be laterally based, while the ones in more risk-averse organizations are typically hierarchical. Furthermore, networks are more formal in hierarchical firms than in ones based on meritocracies. Formally recognized networks for helping outsider-insiders get to the right place at the right time fit with BigFab's hierarchical, authorization culture. It's all right to have senior people help junior ones navigate through the organization. In contrast, such support must be behind the scenes at HiTech since the meritocratic culture expects outsider-insiders to find their own opportunities. As a result, organizational culture influences how networks are developed and managed to match outsider-insiders to critical business challenges.

Sponsors as Matchmakers

Sponsors act as brokers in finding appropriate job assignments for outsider-insiders. Few senior-level sponsors are privy to all the challenges that exist within their organizations, but they have their own extensive networks that can be tapped to facilitate the matchmaking process. Generally, problems percolate up to sponsors by way of conversations with various members of their organization. When they see or hear about a challenge that needs an outsider's perspective, they have the influence to suggest that certain outsider-insiders are the best individuals to address a particular challenge. Even in organizations like HiTech, sponsors such as Dan play a key role in getting outsider-insiders into assignments where they can use their two hats to help solve organizational challenges. This strategic placement of working-level outsider-insiders can be done either formally or informally.

When the challenge requires collaboration or building bridges across functional groups, as it has been in many of the examples throughout this book, sponsors may strategically place outsider-insiders in functions outside their direct line of responsibility. In this case, they may need a cosponsor to provide advocacy and protection for outsider-insiders beyond their chain of command. As one outsider-insider, an engineer who moved into marketing, worried, "Who's my sponsor that is going to look after me while I'm there? It's going to be a stretch for me to go out into marketing and I might fail—I need a bungee cord, to pull me back."

At BigFab, the bungee cord was a group of executives who were each assigned one developing outsider-insider and met quarterly to discuss how their protégés were doing. Such a network affords an umbrella of protection for developing outsider-insiders across functions and divisions. After all, in hierarchical, authorization cultures, advocates typically need to be individuals with executive clout. The executive network also provides an avenue for the executives to learn about available talent to tap. An executive commented, "We are helping them move and grow within BigFab. I know some are ready to move. It is easy to get lost in the system so the network is great. I'm looking to hire someone, and I want someone with a different perspective. I need someone to look at the big picture, not just the mechanics. The network lets me know who is available."

While organizations need outsider-insider advocates who can tap working-level outsider-insiders and get them to the right place at the right time to work on (micro) problems related to macro-level issues, this support can be misinterpreted by some insiders. As we saw at Electronics, when there is heavy reliance on advocacy by executives, many can perceive this action as sponsors trying to push their ideas on the organization. The difference between executive pushing and pulling is whether others perceive that strategically placed outsider-insiders are being assigned to work on a micro challenge aligned with organizational needs. In Dan's case, he had a macro challenge and then found outsider-insiders with the right competencies to help address it.

On the surface, the use of advocates appears to run counter to the current trend of telling employees that they need to manage their own careers and find their own job opportunities. But positions with micro-level challenges where outsider-insiders can apply their two hats are seldom listed as such on formal job posting announcements. Managers typically think they need just a specific skill set, not outsider perspectives. Granted, outsider-insider hiring managers may recognize that they need kindred souls to help them identify micro-level challenges to pull in new ideas, but that is not something that is broadly communicated to insiders. An outsider-insider in a large, risk-averse organization observed, "You're expected to fend for yourself. On the one hand, I say, 'That's all right. We should be able to make a place for ourselves.' The other part of me says, 'This is a very political organization, and you need someone to help you meet the right people and get in the right positions.'"

Organizations tend to manage this trade-off through a simultaneous reliance on competency and advocacy. Competency is used as the basis for evaluating performance and recognizing talent, while advocacy provides a mechanism to help developing outsider-insiders maneuver through the organization and find a place that can best use their two hats.

In many respects, advocacy reflects how things work, as one manager summed up how hiring decisions are made: "If there are two people whose performances are equal, the one who is a known entity will get the job. It is human nature. The manager is betting his career on the people whom he hires, and he wants someone he knows can do the job." As much as most people want to believe that objectivity rules in the selection of individuals to fill specific job opportunities, in fact there is always an element of subjectivity: advocates "suggest" what should happen. It helps to have a sponsor who will put a good word in for a candidate, especially when the hiring manager does not personally know a particular outsider-insider.

As individuals move up the organization, competency should and typically does supplant advocacy. But how the balance between advocacy and competency plays out and when competency begins to kick in and supplant advocacy is linked to an organization's culture: the more entrepreneurial, the less formal the advocacy. But even in very entrepreneurial organizations, informal sponsors help to identify or design opportunities for developing outsider-insiders to learn and succeed in the organization. An outsider-insider within one of the entrepreneurial companies described, "You have a sense that there is an invisible hand guiding you and that there are con-versations about you behind closed doors." But these sponsors, such as the "godparents" at HiTech, are merely coaches, with final deci-sions around appropriate matches left up to the individual. And in keeping with the company's meritocratic environment, sponsorship is solely based on performance; outstanding performance on a job leads to recognition and confidence that an individual is worthy of being watched over. Sponsorship is not handed to someone just because he or she has been given a development opportunity. Once developing outsider-insiders demonstrate their potential, sponsors step in and informally help them find opportunities that will have an impact. Often this sponsorship comes in the form of visibility relative to an individual's competence in introducing new ideas as opposed to a suggestion that a particular outsider-insider should be placed in a specific assignment.

In contrast, BigFab relies more heavily on advocacy, as evi-denced by its executive network of sponsors who help get outsider-insiders to the right place at the right time to find opportunities to pull in change. Although the company is attempting to reduce its dependency on advocacy, deep roots exist in a legacy system of strong sponsorship. Given the hierarchical and authorization nature of the culture, many developing outsider-insiders believe that it is still necessary to have influential advocates who can pro-vide authorization to their outsider ideas. This view, however, is not universal. One outsider-insider argued that "every time you use that leverage you are weakening a brick in your foundation." But even this individual recognized the need to have someone willing to take a chance on a "short-timer" in BigFab's experience-based culture.

Advocacy also provides a bit of protection for outsider-insiders when they observe gaps between current assumptions and the root cause of challenges they encounter. Over the years, BigFab's mid-dle managers have been conditioned to resist tinkering with the status quo. As such, outsider-insiders are often perceived as a threat. As one manager noted, "Peter was new to the area. I spent one year introducing him. It took a special effort to put him into one of our oldest plants. It is a hierarchical organization. I end up providing air cover for many like Peter." But as would be expected, once outsider-insiders illustrate how their unique competencies can be of value to BigFab, "air cover" is no longer needed, and the competency model kicks in. As another manager noted, "If you look at more senior people, you find that the higher they got in the hierarchy, the advocacy started to fade. At that point competency starts to kick in."

As a critical mass of outsider-insiders climbs up into the senior ranks, they in turn became matchmakers and use their networks to be advocates for those who follow. This has become a win-win for the organization and the outsider-insiders. As one of BigFab's executive outsider-insiders put it, "The network helps the younger people learn about the organization. It helps me find people to work for me to help make change. It's like a pyramid that builds upon itself." The effectiveness of the network matching was validated by one newly developed outsider-insider who returned from full immersion on the outside and proclaimed, "I was able to take what I learned and apply it right away."

Network Mentors

Mentors or coaches also can function as network navigators. They help the people whom they advise learn the ropes: who does what, who has influence on what, and who to go to in order to get things done. "I'm a network guy," said one manager. "I'd tell him, 'Go see this one, talk to that one, go on over there and see these couple of guys.'" By sharing their network, mentors help build their protégé's network; in return, they reap the benefit of a new network link.

As with other elements of the support infrastructure, it takes time to cultivate outsider-insider networks. Networks build as careers progress. So early on, developing outsider-insiders need help finding the necessary links to build support for their outsider perspectives. They need to rely on the goodwill of their supporters and advisers to develop their network. As one new employee recalled,

> The plant manager was not an easy person to convince on the need for technological change. It ended up that I sold him by selling the people who would work with the technology, and they sold him on the idea. My supervisor gave me those people. I would have never been able to find those people without his help, but then it was easy to convince them of the benefits of the change and they convinced the plant manager. My supervisor taught me how he had sold some of his projects, and through him I learned how to sell change from the bottom up using internal networks.

This supervisor not only shared his network to help this new recruit find other more seasoned outsider-insiders but also coached the developing outsider-insider in how to leverage the culture.

As we saw in Chapter Six, the degree to which organizations formalize mentoring relationships tends to be culturally based. By and large, the more entrepreneurial an organization is, the less inclined it will be to implement a formal structure with assigned mentors. Risk-averse organizations, however, often have a more formal, top-down mentoring process. One such company created a mentorship program where an outside vendor matches mentors to mentees based on a variety of factors. Mentors and their assigned mentees attend parallel training sessions and then meet at a reception. By design, the mentors are not part of the individual's performance management or career development, so there can be an open dialogue without fear of reprisal. This also automatically adds another network link outside the developing outsider-insider's chain of command.

Appointed mentors tend to be like blind dates: both parties must determine whether to pursue a relationship. In many hierarchical companies, as is the case in some parts of the world, arranged marriages are the norm. But like all other unions, some work, some persevere, and others disintegrate. In other words, some mentor-mentee relationships work well, while others end up being mediocre at best. As a result, many companies engage in a perennial debate about the appropriateness and effectiveness of assigning mentors. Not surprisingly, the best coaching relationship is that between two people who like and respect one another. There is a chemistry that translates into friendship. Such advice and counsel can come in many different forms and serve many different purposes. One of BigFab's developing outsider-insiders summed it up well:

I have had four different types of mentors, all at the same time. They come in all flavors and levels of the company. The first one was the VP of the division. I used to talk to him about specific topics like career development and stuff like that, my learning experiences, what's happening. I guess we made commitments to each other. He would call this or that person and make him aware of who I was and what I was doing. He sort of said, "I'll keep an eye on you." He was high enough in the company to talk about things and not conjecture. If something was going to happen, he could make it happen. The information he had was not third hand. . . . We did not spend much time talking about specific learning. It was more like, "What do you need?" My second mentor had real knowledge in operations. He is very aggressive, very demanding. When you disagree with him, he is very straightforward about things. He'll say, "If you can't do it, I will find someone else." He was good to me, but he kept me from making my work area my playground. To him, a schedule is important and the customer comes first. My third mentor, I could sit down anytime with him and he would always talk to me. We had some real mind-expanding sessions, along with management sessions. He allowed us to do anything, to stretch the limits. You know, go outside the box and think about new things. We would just do blue skies for a while. My fourth mentor was probably my most important one. He is my peer; we work together. I guess he is a type of personal mentor. He's got a character that I want to emulate. He has a real balance and understands about valuing people and products. He knows how to use people as a resource. We talk about personal issues with each other. We mentor each other.

The result of all this mentoring is a network that functions much like the sponsor network. As challenges arise that need outsider-insider perspectives, these mentors become matchmakers. Even if they do not have the necessary clout to influence the match directly, they can use their own network nodes to get the message to executives who own the challenge. And as the organization builds a critical mass of people who can wear two hats, these individuals become a strong network looking for gaps and identifying additional opportunities for their fellow outsider-insiders. Eventually, as these outsider-insiders rise through the organization, they become role models and mentors for developing outsider-insiders who follow them, and the network continues to grow.

Managing the Dark Side of Advocacy

At the same time, strong mentorship can be particularly deadly for outsider-insiders if they and their organizations blindly assume that all sponsorship and mentorship is goodness. As we have seen, formal mentors and sponsors are considered a crutch in meritocracies. And even in organizations that depend on a formal advocacy model, there is a potential for resentment from peers who do not receive the same levels of support. But one of the most deadly aspects of advocacy is revealed when an overreliance on the guidance and goodwill of the sponsors or mentors leads to a loss of independent thinking, the one thing that outsider-insiders must continually work to maintain. Having advocates who are themselves outsider-insiders helps to minimize potential negative effects because these people understand what it is like to be an outsider-insider and are more attuned to the need to nurture outsider perspectives. But even so, when protégés spend time learning the philosophy of their mentors or sponsors, they are likely to internalize that manner of thinking and to act according to its tenets. Some of the potential unintended consequences of advocacy are summarized in Table 7.1. With planning and discussion around expectations and roles, most of the pitfalls can be avoided, but it is

Table 7.1. The Dark Side of Advocacy

	Sponsors	*Mentors*
Limit diversity	Tendency to select protégés who think like an advocate	Tendency to mold or be molded by advice and counsel
Pacing	Potential to monitor pace or restrict opportunities	Reluctance to counter advice of mentor
Misfit	Advocate loses organizational clout	Lack of chemistry between mentor and protégé

critical to keep these in mind. Both organizations and individual outsider-insiders must be conscious of and jointly fight against the dark side of advocacy.

Limiting Diversity of Mental Models

While advocacy helps outsider-insiders find opportunities to introduce outsider perspectives, the process can backfire. Outsider-insiders tend to gravitate to kindred souls. It is human nature to feel comfortable with people who look, speak, and behave like oneself. As a result, the process of sponsorship can lead to insularity and the loss of one's outsider hat, a subject we explore further in Chapter Eight.

A similar problem can arise from intensive mentoring. Having had extensive experience in the type of work that protégés are doing, mentors typically offer valuable advice, help define goals, supply information on developments within the company, and provide visibility and recommendations for their protégés. In return, protégés learn from their mentors by asking questions and discussing potential problems. Protégés typically reciprocate by following their mentors' advice and, in essence, following in their footsteps. Perpetuating a mentor's legacy, unfortunately, can narrow one's mental models unless part of the mentor's philosophy is always to wear two hats and continually convey that message, including being willing to confront each other's assumptions.

Pacing

Sponsors invest their personal time and energy in developing outside-insiders. Although they want to see their protégés succeed and have an impact on the organization, there is no guarantee of reciprocity—that they will share their "offspring." As a result, when sponsors are faced with key challenges that need outsider perspectives and they are pleased with an individual's ability to help implement new ideas, they may be reluctant to let their protégé move on to other parts of the organization. As one outsider-insider recalled, "I was offered a promotion into another group. They called me first and asked if I'd be interested. I didn't want to upset anyone, so I told them to go through the proper channels. After a while, [I learned that my boss] had turned down the offer for me. . . . I guess I was a little flattered that they wanted to keep me."

This individual's situation illustrates how outsider-insiders can end up being subject to the speed at which their advocates feel they are ready or are willing to sponsor them in jobs that have broader impact. Many protégés are also reluctant to seek advice elsewhere or try to expand their experiences because any or all of these actions might be viewed as a betrayal of one's mentor. As a result, they end up self-limiting their activities in order to avoid offending their mentor. Another outsider-insider lamented, "There were people who told me that it would be a bad thing for me to say no to him, so when he told me to take this job, I felt I had to."

Finally, there is the potential for some fallout if advocates try to help, but the outsider-insider's immediate chain of command interprets the assistance as meddling. One outsider-insider recalled, "I've been kind of lucky. I've had someone fairly high up as a mentor. We met nearly every week. I made suggestions to him about things. One time he went to the plant manager about my suggestions. After that, the plant manager didn't want me to talk to this mentor anymore."

Examples such as the ones above can often be avoided through up-front, open dialogue between the parties. Many advocates believe they are doing what is in the best interest of their protégé, but sometimes those actions may run counter to the desires of the developing outsider-insiders. Having several sponsors and mentors, like the BigFab outsider-insider with four advisers, can also help to alleviate some of these issues. Multiple inputs tend to help developing outsider-insiders recognize when a sponsor may be overprotective or not providing the specific type of guidance that may be needed in specific situations. If and when any one adviser begins limiting an individual's ability to introduce outsider perspectives, an outsider-insider with multiple advisers then has alternative avenues to seek advice and help in strategizing how to address issues in a way that does not alienate the sponsor at fault. In doing so, it is important for the developing outsider-insiders to be as clear as they can be about the type of advocacy they would like to receive from each mentor or sponsor. But as one senior outsider-insider recalled, it is often difficult to know what it is one wants early in one's career:

> The problem is that some [protégés] ask in a way that is too open ended—like, "I'm a blank slate, come help." You have to be more directed and tell people specifically the problem you have and what type of help you need. . . . I had a lot of meetings with my mentor around career advice. In the early meetings, I was clueless. He would ask, "What do you want to know?" and I didn't know. You need to learn how to use those interactions.

This is where having an adviser who has previously gone through the development process is extremely helpful.

Potential Misfit

There are several potential types of misfits, most of which are more likely to occur in organizations where advocates are assigned as opposed to being self-initiated by either the advocate or protégé.

One manager likened it to a "dating process. We can encourage mentoring, but we can't force it." One unfortunate outcome of any matchmaking process is a lack of chemistry: the two parties just don't like each other. Ideally the relationship should be one that is chosen by both the mentor and the protégé, but some formal advocacy systems become programmatic and do not provide any mechanism for self-selection. All too often, mentors and their assigned protégés feel obligated to continue to meet to check off a box on a form. But as one outsider-insider noted, this only leads to frustration on both sides. "I'm not sure I liked my mentor. We used to meet every couple of months and discuss how things were going, but the personality was not there. . . . There is not so much learning there as listening to experts. . . . It is very frustrating."

One contributing factor can be a shortage of outsider-insider advocates who clearly understand what it means to be a sponsor or mentor. As a result, developing outsider-insiders, especially in organizations that have formal advocacy systems, end up being teamed with individuals who lack the skills or clout to be truly effective advocates. Worse yet, "advocates" may be traditional insiders who do not value outsider perspectives.

Moreover, all advocates are not equal in influence or commitment to their protégés. Those who evolve out of prior relationships and choose to be advocates have a vested interest in making their protégés as successful as possible. Others, however, are just assigned a protégé: to the developing outsider-insider, it can appear that they have just been provided a random advocate. In many cases, the latter tend to have less investment in their advisee. Unfortunately, both sets of protégés often compare the level of advocacy they receive, and the assigned ones often end up resenting those who have been tapped on the shoulder. In the worst-case scenario, an advocate can actually become a liability, particularly when this person loses organizational clout. This is particularly troublesome if the developing outsider-insider has failed to build a network of other sponsors and mentors.

Finally, there are times when a relationship sours and there is no easy way to walk away from the established pairings. This is particularly difficult for protégés who either disagree with their advocate or feel that they are not getting anything from the relationship. But a seasoned outsider-insider advised that it is important not to bad-mouth people who are trying to be helpful:

> People will help you if you honor their contribution. You have to respect what they have done. Senior leaders are the same. Their fingerprints are everywhere. You can't discount forty years of their life. If you recognize what they have done and don't just come in and say how screwed up the things they have done are, they want to make you successful. You are a reflection of them. I never say a bad thing about my boss. Even when I feel compelled to I don't. I can argue with them but never bad-mouth them.

When Matchmaking Works

Despite the potential for the dark side to rear its ugly head, matchmaking does work. The best antidote for avoiding the dark side is awareness of its existence and continual vigilance in maintaining outsider perspectives on the part of advocates and protégés so both parties are able to step back and be open to alternative perspectives, the subject of the final chapter. But first, as a counter to the dark side, we end this chapter with an example of matchmaking as an essential element to a success story: new ideas were pulled in to deal with seemingly intractable challenges, which ultimately created the true change that revitalized a waning manufacturing facility. In this case, one individual (a senior-level outsider-insider) played the part of both sponsor and mentor to a developing outsider-insider.

Rob, a member of the corporate technology improvement group in a traditional risk-averse organization, was an ideal candidate waiting for an opportunity to put his outsider concepts to work. He had recently graduated from an advanced degree program in manufacturing that had included a six-month internship in one of his corporation's oldest facilities that had not seen change in the past twenty to thirty years. The plant was doing very poorly on almost all accounts. Rob described the environment he found:

> It was a very proud place, profitable, talented, and had a lot of tra-
> dition as a plant. In fact, we call it the Fortress. Those who have
> been successful in the past were too proud to want to hear anything
> that was not their invention. The operation was performing poorly
> and tried to cover up most of the problems. The concept of wearing
> two hats, an insider and an outsider, had not registered with most of
> the managers.

Shortly after Rob completed his internship assignment, the plant's engineering manager, Ted, was assigned the role of production manager with the expressed mandate to turn the plant around. Ted was a typical outsider-insider, willing to shift functions and move out of his comfortable technical world to help address a major challenge. And like most other outsider-insiders, he was constantly searching for new and different approaches. In one of his searches, he came across Rob's graduate thesis on inventory improvement processes. As Ted recalled, he learned about Rob through his network:

> I had heard about [Rob's program] through one of my prior bosses. I
> was the engineering manager, and I was researching supply chain
> management. One of my engineers suggested I read Rob's thesis.
> Four months later I became the production manager. I asked to
> have Rob come work for me. He had been hired in to the corporate
> planning group, and he moved to the plant. I liked his thoughts and
> ideas of how to add value through the process.

Rob, with Ted as his mentor, plotted out a plan to introduce new approaches to managing inventory within the operation. First, they divided the plant into sections (flow paths) and began to get employees to focus on where value was added in each path. Rob recognized that his first step was to help *the plant* realize that they had an inventory problem, that is, he could not push his ideas on the workforce. He explained his approach to the pulling change process:

> The first step to learning or to change is to accept that there is a problem, then envision solutions, and then implementation. If they don't admit the problems, forget about helping them. So for me, in trying to help them solve problems and inject any knowledge or wisdom, I only focused on the problems that they were willing to admit. Even to get to this stage, it took a lot of trust building and required a lot of relationship building. I didn't have the power to force them to admit the problems they had, although we could have proposed some.

At 7:30 A.M. each day, a production employee from every "path" reported on how the section did the previous day and outlined the efforts being made to reduce inventory. The plant was used to weekly production meetings but had never tracked inventory on a daily basis. Once improvements within each flow path were achieved, employees were able to begin tackling barriers to reducing inventory between departments. Over time, the new procedures and routines became embedded in a new set of organizational assumptions. As Ted noted, "It was demonstrated skills with measurable results. Rob was doing the work, providing the ideas and concepts, and I was the buffer using my experience. People quickly recognized Rob's unique skill set and he was willing to openly share."

In a sense, Rob's success is easy to explain. He had a significant problem that needed immediate attention and had the knowledge of how to fix the problem. But Rob didn't just come in with his solution. Although he knew what needed to be done, he carefully set the stage and waited for just the right moment to introduce those pieces of the solution that people could apply to see improvements. Furthermore, Rob and Ted were a perfect team: Rob had the expertise, and Ted had the organizational power to support Rob. Even if Ted had been the inventory expert and knew everything that Rob knew, he still would have needed Rob to identify the daily challenges at the shop floor level. Rob too could not have done it alone since he lacked the organizational power and credibility needed to focus attention on the change effort.

One of Ted's objectives in bringing Rob into the operation was for him to train others within the plant and leverage his skills, and Rob delivered. His approach created a network of employees, the flow path representatives who reported in each morning, who became his ambassadors looking for opportunities for further inventory improvements. In this way, the plant created lots of little "pings" that reverberated into a "pong" to improve plant performance and instill new assumptions around inventory management.

Chapter Eight

Maintaining Outsider-Insider Perspectives

Remaining an outsider-insider over time is not a simple matter. It is something that an individual needs continually to decide to do and an organization must continually systematically support to do: true change happens, ultimately, when these two commitments are in tandem. As one outsider-insider struggling to maintain a personal equilibrium proclaimed, "It's like two liquids that don't mix!" For many people, the two hats don't mix easily, which is why many of them are one-shot outsider-insiders: they perceive a challenge where change could be "pulled in," seek and support an alternative approach to solve the challenge, and then fall back into a groove of wearing only one hat. Sometimes the outsider hat succumbs to internal demands; other times the insider hat just doesn't fit anymore as an organization evolves in different directions than a particular outsider-insider prefers. Not everyone wants to or should strive to be a perpetual outsider-insider, but there are people who do, and organizations benefit from having a cadre of them being systematically aligned to macro challenges and continually available for seeking gaps between organizational assumptions and the root causes of challenges they encounter. Maintaining this twin perspective requires individuals able to live in two worlds over time. This, in turn, requires constant vigilance on the part of both outsider-insiders and their organizations to ensure that the two hats stay blended in the right proportions.

Individuals can easily fall into the same rut as organizations do: their observations and analyses can become clouded by personal assumptions or mental models. Thus, outsider-insiders must be willing to follow, on a personal level, a path like the one we have taken throughout this book: they must be willing to take on this role, and they must be supported in doing so. When introducing alternative perspectives, outsider-insiders must be cognizant of challenges to their own assumptions as well, however, and that is a focus of this chapter. Sometimes outsider-insiders can become so fixated on a gap in assumptions that they miss an opportunity to pull in outsider perspectives, or they may attempt to introduce new ideas and their approach backfires because they are too headstrong in their approach. In other words, their own assumption about the approach they are using to help others see alternative perspectives can itself become as much of a problem as the one they are trying to address: they cannot see the forest for the trees because they are unwilling to step back and question their own approach. When this happens, the real challenge can be obscured, and they, rather than the challenge, become the lightning rod.

Questioning one's own assumptions is part of personal growth and development—an essential but sometimes painful maturation process. When it happens to outsider-insiders, it can throw the two hats out of balance. Organizations must be on the lookout for when this occurs and not just assume that outsider-insiders will automatically be prepared and eager to attack new challenges that endlessly come along. Similarly, outsider-insiders should not take for granted that they can retain their ability to bridge the outside and inside worlds without putting in time and effort to maintain their own equilibrium, regardless of what happens to them as part of their growth and development. Neither organization nor individual outsider-insider is fixed in place.

In keeping with the theme of dual responsibility that we have seen throughout this book, this final step of outsider-insider personal development process points out that this is not a solo journey. Organizations can help their outsider-insiders by providing ongoing support to keep the two hats healthy and in harmony with one another. The support infrastructure does not stop when outsider-insiders get to the right place at the right time to pull change. If it did, it would create one-shot outsider-insiders. So in this final chapter, we explore how outsider-insiders and their organizations nurture and maintain the wearing of two hats over time. As you will hear from the veteran outsider-insiders we tracked, the journey is often both frustrating and exhilarating.[1]

Living in Two Worlds over Time

Holding on to outsider views is not easy in organizations with deeply engrained cultures. Without support and protection, many outsider-insiders revert to being insiders under the constant pressure to conform to insider norms. As one outsider-insider noted, "I have to struggle with how to maintain an outside perspective and still be an insider. I don't want to become bogged down by the bureaucracy or confused by the standard operating procedures." It takes personal stamina and strong belief systems to continually seek ways to introduce alternative perspectives. When asked what keeps her going, one veteran outsider-insider explained, "It's a personal belief that it really can be better."

One of the dilemmas of repeatedly identifying gaps and introducing new concepts is that outsider-insiders build a history within their organizations. Success in getting others to recognize gaps and introduce alternative ways of doing things affects how others perceive outsider-insiders, both good and bad. On the positive side, they become known as expert problem solvers and are called in to address increasingly bigger and more important challenges. But arrogance can creep in on the part of both organizations and the outsider-insiders: these people become "the" problem solvers. Underlying this perception is a dangerous assumption: that their competencies or tool kits will be sufficient to identify the root cause of any challenge being faced. When and if there is a mismatch, outsider-insiders need an extended network to tap for alternative approaches, or they may need further development activities to refresh their outsider hats.

Success can also breed discontent, particularly if outsider-insiders become superstars within their organizations. Insiders may resent the attention bestowed on proactive outsider-insiders and view them as troublemakers constantly going against the status quo. As one senior outsider-insider put it, "After a while you become famous, or infamous, for doing out-of-the-box things. You create an image for yourself. Unknowingly, you end up creating a hostile relationship with people who are not inclined to change. These are the people who sit on the sidelines and are upset with the changes you are suggesting."

Continual attacks from the corporate immune system cause wear and tear on the two hats. Some outsider-insiders thrive on the challenge, but many succumb to pressures from their work associates. They give up and fall back into the culture, or they find more comfort in their outsider hat and gradually move further and further off center, or they leave the company.

Individuals mature, as do organizations. Life changes—marriage or divorce, children, health problems, a death in the family—are times of personal reflection that lead us to reexamine our values and personal assumptions. These events can cause outsider-insiders to fall out of sync with their organization's priorities and personal demands. Some outsider-insiders find that they aren't comfortable with wearing the insider hat. They may have thought that they would fit in when they entered the organization and may have even built sufficient credibility to become an insider, at least to other insiders. But discomfort with certain aspects of a culture can build up over time and make it difficult for these people to live within the organization and be true to themselves. One outsider-insider observed, "I know a couple of people who remained outsiders and have had a hard time wearing that second hat. Some of them feel it is a betrayal of their ideals and can't cope with doing things the way we do them."

Wearing and keeping the insider hat can be especially difficult for outsider-insiders who work virtually and are not physically located on the inside. It is often easy to lose sight of inside assumptions when surrounded by outside influences. Even if they have made the transition to remote work after spending a number of years internally, there is an added burden of not losing touch and maintaining linkages with people on the inside, similar to what developing outsider-insiders must do when they go for full immersion on the outside.

The message is that being a perpetual outsider-insider is an unnatural state; it is not a self-perpetuating flame. Outsider-insiders and their organizations must proactively find ways to keep outsider perspectives alive and in balance with insider needs. It requires lifelong learning and revisiting many of the development activities we explored in Chapter Five in helping insiders to recognize how organizational assumptions can be the root cause of challenges they face. The only difference here is that the challenges are now personal in addition to being organizational.

Competing Forces

One of the difficulties in maintaining a balance between the two hats is that there are what appear to be competing forces in operation. Being able to continually wear two hats and step back as an outsider to objectively analyze the root cause of inside challenges requires an inquisitive, open mind. But once outsider-insiders identify gaps between existing assumptions and the root cause they observe, it takes perseverance, often in the face of adversity, to get others to see where internal assumptions are in fact the problem. Tradi-tionally, those two characteristics—open-mindedness and perseverance—have been at odds with each other. Perseverance requires holding on to strong convictions in the face of adversity, which translates into being convinced that your assumptions are correct. As one outside-insider executive noted, "You need to have confidence in what you believe in, to be able to embody, evaluate, and transcend the culture in the organization." But sticking to one's guns can run counter to questioning one's own assumptions, which is pivotal to maintaining objectivity as either outsider or insider. Another outsider-insider observed, "Thinking that you know something so resolutely closes off alternative opportunities."

The solution to this apparent contradiction is in the sequencing. First, outsider-insiders must use an open mind to identify gaps, and then they need to be patient and persistent in helping others to recognize those gaps and accept alternative approaches. This can be a bit confusing since wearing two hats is a simultaneous activity—being on the inside but at the same time looking at a situation through an outsider's lens. So it is an acquired skill that outsider-insiders must practice and hone to be able to make a seamless transition back and forth from the left- to the right-hand side of Figure 8.1. They must be adept at knowing when to question assumptions and when to stick to what they believe is true. And to complicate matters, it is also a two-phase process: first at an organizational level, then at a personal one.

This book has focused on being able and willing to question organizational assumptions, but in so doing, outsider-insiders must also examine their own personal beliefs; after all, they are part insider. However, if they continue to question their assumptions even after they have identified a gap, they can get caught in analysis paralysis and never get anything done. So once they are convinced that insider assumptions are at fault, the execution stage begins. At this point, perseverance is of paramount importance. Yet

Figure 8.1. Balancing Competing Forces

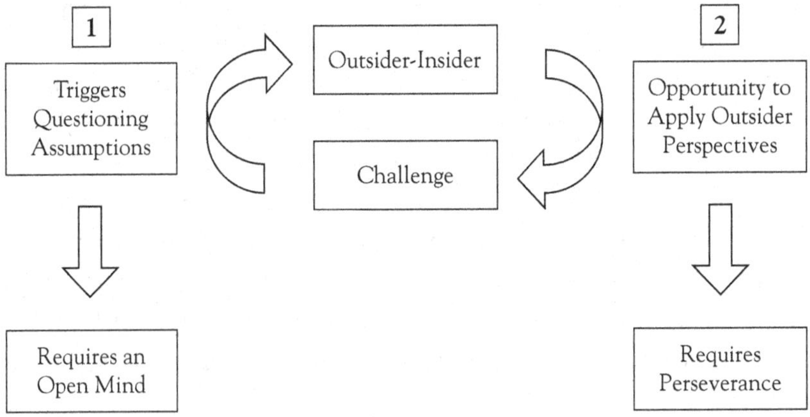

sticking to one's beliefs can be painful in the face of stiff resistance. A veteran outsider-insider reflected:

> You have to be able to tolerate incredible pain. Even in the ideal world, people just don't accept change. In my career, there have been several times when I thought I was going to get fired, and I probably would have if I panicked. But I didn't panic, and I stuck with my beliefs and made it through difficult situations. My career would have been over if I hadn't. I survived and demonstrated that I could tolerate the pain and demonstrated I could take it.

A portion of the pain can be mitigated by continually cycling back through the two-step process depicted in Figure 8.1, this time looking for personal rather than organizational gaps. Even when outsider-insiders are confident in their analysis of the root cause and the alternative steps that will rectify the challenge they face, their own approach may now be an auxiliary challenge— and the source of the resistance. Another veteran outsider-insider recognized that it takes personal reflection and a constant self-reminder that challenges come in many different forms, sometimes personal:

> I have to constantly remind myself that what is obvious to me is not obvious to others. I don't mean that in an arrogant way. I just realize that I have to help others see why I see things the way I do. It takes patience, and I find I have to coach myself. I have to take the time to really understand why I believe things are the way they are so I can explain it to others. I find I get personally frustrated because others don't get it, and then I have to start coaching myself and ask myself, "How well am I articulating what I want to be saying?" If I'm not, I can't be frustrated at them. I start saying, "Why don't people get it?" You just have to recognize that you have to step them through it. You have to keep at it and help them see things differently. And even if they get it conceptually, they sometimes can't put it into action.

This outsider-insider was willing to cycle repeatedly between questioning assumptions and perseverance as many times as needed to help others see gaps and accept alternative ways of doing things. Hence, living in two worlds over time requires both inquisitiveness and stick-to-itiveness. For some, these appear to be competing forces, but for perpetual outsider-insiders, they are just two competencies in the outsider-insider toolbox, there to use at the right moment. The toolbox, however, needs periodic realignment and replenishment— what I call outsider-insider preventive maintenance.

Outsider-Insider Preventive Maintenance

Becoming a perpetual outsider-insider is, as I have repeatedly stressed, not a onetime phenomenon for either the individual or the organization. It is a process that requires continual attention. "I have to fight every day not to lose my outsider perspectives," a persistent outsider-insider said. "It's a struggle every day to keep my beliefs intact." For this outsider-insider and others, one way to ease the struggle is for the organization to build a groundswell of support that creates the "pong" to embed new ways of thinking across the organization. When that occurs, individual outsider-insiders feel less like a lone voice in the wilderness. But once organizations have built a critical mass of support for alternative perspectives and outsider-insiders have succeeded in finding recurring opportunities to pull in aligned outsider perspectives, those new ways of doing things become part of the insider fabric. That's the good news. But success can also breed complacency. Outsider-insiders need continual stimuli to avoid becoming insular.

Organizations need to provide regularly scheduled outsider-insider maintenance, much like preventive maintenance on equipment. As with equipment, there is no one set plan that fits every outsider-insider. Some need very little stimuli; others need regularly scheduled renewal activities, much like the jolts that insiders need when learning to wear two hats. Outsider-insider refresher events are similar to the development activities discussed in Chapter Five.

The external jolts need not be as significant, however. Once outsider-insiders have learned to wear two hats, it is like riding a bicycle. They just need to get back on and practice a bit: they need an exercise regimen to keep in shape and be ready for the upcoming, but as yet unidentified, challenges. Hence, outsider-insider preventive maintenance plans should include structured time to reflect on both personal and organizational assumptions and periodic "redipping" activities that expose outsider-insiders to outsider perspectives.

Rejuvenating Outsider Perspectives

Outsider-insiders are typically people who thrive on new adventures; they are constantly in search of new opportunities to put their outsider hats to work. Unfortunately, tenure in a job can stifle inquisitiveness. Furthermore, obvious gaps get closed, and the ones that remain may in part be a result of things outsider-insiders have influenced. Hence, the longer one is in a job, the more "ingrained" one can become. One outsider-insider outlined the problem:

> The longer time I spend in a role, the more I get sucked into it and lose my outside perspective. I was in one job for four years and I remember coming in with a ton of ideas. Over time, I got more ingrained in the nuts and bolts of the job. Then I changed jobs and had a lot of new ideas. So if you draw an x-y diagram, initially you start off high on the chart and then tend to taper off.

Every new job offers a chance to search for opportunities to pull in outsider points of view. It is like starting anew as an outsider and seeing things that test mental models about why people behave as they do. And since many job changes end up being across functions, businesses, or locations, each new assignment enables outsider-insiders to apply lessons learned from prior roles and spread their outsider perspectives across the organization.

Obviously, constant job rotations carry a risk. As we saw at Electronics, outsider-insiders can become viewed as "high maintenance" by immediate managers and peers. Some developing outsider-insiders make the mistake of using short-term assignments to introduce new ideas and move on before the entire pulling change process is complete. A veteran outsider-insider observed, "You need to improve things that really make a difference in the long term. Very smart people quickly learn that they can look good by setting the bar low, picking the low-hanging fruit, and then getting out before any long-term things come to bear. I've learned over the years that if you don't do the right thing, you end up leaving people worse off than before." Hence, organizations need to provide preventive maintenance activities that will rejuvenate outsider perspectives without having to continuously move outsider-insiders to new jobs. An alternative is to look to short-term excursions on the outside, similar to the one we saw in Chapter Five, that test both personal and organizational assumptions.

An essential component for maintaining balance is finding time for reflection. An outsider-insider earlier noted that it is easy to get immersed in the nuts and bolts of an assignment. There is little time for stepping back and reflecting as we saw with insiders learning to wear two hats. With organizations reducing staff to be "lean and mean," finding time to balance work and family is difficult. Daily demands require speedy responses. Taking time to reflect on what is happening is typically viewed as countercultural. It's not considered "real work." As a result, reflection time is a luxury often left for annual vacations. But once a year is not frequent enough; reflection must be an ongoing, integrated exercise discipline. As one executive outsider-insider discovered, getting away from the daily grind, even if it was just a change of venue, is a way to see things in a different light:

One of my strengths is that I am a strong results-oriented person, probably to a fault. But sometimes I need to step back and say, "What are we doing here?" I've noticed that anytime I am out of the plant for a few days, I see things differently when I come back. It's the boiled frog thing: every day you're surrounded with urgent things that need to be done and you don't have time to rise above the urgent demands. You need to look at the big picture and not get bogged down with the details.

Another outsider-insider found that benchmarking another company, especially in a totally different industry, can jolt one's "assumptions about what fits or doesn't fit back home." Provided one makes the journey with an inquisitive mind, it is an opportunity for reflection and dusting off the organizational cobwebs that have accumulated.

Interactions with developing outsider-insiders can also present an opportunity for personal reflection. Effective mentoring serves as a dual support system for both mentors and mentees. Developing outsider-insiders act as windows for their mentors, enabling them to see gaps in generational assumptions—another form of cultural blinders. As one executive outsider-insider noted, mentoring helps him maintain an appropriate balance between his two hats:

> An element of it is the enemy is us. I've been here long enough and I've been a part of decisions. . . . Serving as a mentor for people who are younger helps to maintain an outsider frame. You are constantly being given frames that are different from yours. I'm being challenged with, "This is totally screwed up," and I have to keep myself from being defensive and try to understand what is happening and understand their perspective.

Similarly, interviewing job candidates, especially ones fresh out of college, is another avenue for tapping into new ways of thinking and making time for reflection. Interviewees tend to ask probing questions about the culture within the company. This often forces individuals conducting the interviews to step back and reexamine their own values and assumptions, a reminder that "truth in advertising" requires individuals to be honest with themselves while also portraying an honest picture of the organization's environment and macro challenges. One outsider-insider who was part of a campus recruiting team noted, "I learn content from what they have done and also see how people think. It makes me reflect on where I am and what I believe in. They ask me what I like about my job, and it forces me to figure it out. I get energized by coming to campus and doing interviews. The personal reflection is a benefit to me."

Hence, outsider-insider preventive maintenance activities are easily incorporated into "real work" in many ways. It just takes a little extra effort to find ways to make reflection part of daily routines. But there is no guarantee that outsider-insiders will come out refreshed and ready to grapple with the next challenge. Some might find that their outsider hat is their true self and end up being one of those who no longer feel comfortable as an insider. But it is a risk worth taking. Without reflection, outsider-insiders can burn out from the constant firefighting and become insular; the result is a loss of equilibrium. But finding and seeing opportunities to sharpen one's outsider perspectives takes self-discipline and constant reminders and support from other outsider-insiders. Hence, organizations must continually reinforce the value of, and need for, outsider-insider preventive maintenance, especially reflection. This also includes encouraging outsider-insiders to maintain peer networks of fellow outsider-insiders who can help each other maintain a healthy balance between their two hats.

Maintaining Bridges Between the Two Worlds

Maintaining a network of friends who also wear two hats, internally and externally, provides a home within a home for outsider-insiders. Outsider-insiders need dialogue with kindred souls who share a common view of what is possible. As one outsider-insider said, "It is terribly lonely at times. We try to keep a fabric of connections of people to go to. It is so important to have people you trust and can talk to." This fabric is often the result of relationships built during earlier developmental activities or formal networks, like the one at BigFab, that are set up to mentor developing outsider-insiders.

Maintaining bridges to the outside is also necessary. External networks, such as industry groups, professional societies, and alumni groups, provide a continual source of outsider perspectives. One veteran outsider-insider found that working within the local community is another way to broaden connections and explore new horizons:

> I think you can maintain your external perspective, but you have to work at it. You can do it through your network. It's not the same as when you are fresh out, but you can maintain it by going to conferences and talking to folks externally. I'm on the board for the chamber of commerce, and it gives me an opportunity to network with small firms and other companies in the area. But I have to work at it. If you allow yourself to be encased in your job, you become introspective and you lose your external perspective.

Finally, lifelong learning opportunities can end up doing double duty as outsider-insider preventive maintenance activities. As outsider-insiders acquire new skills and perspectives, they expand their external networks. As one outsider-insider experienced after attending an extended coaching course, "I've engaged with a new community of folks who have different ways of relating. I have learned how important it is to have a community—to establish it and keep it alive to institute different ways of thinking. I spend time with them and then come back inside and see the contrast."

Linkages to the outsider world also provide external support groups to buttress internal infrastructures. They can serve as a safe haven for outsider-insiders to commiserate with one another and remind themselves that they really aren't crazy—they just see things differently from others within their organizations.[2] In this regard, one executive outsider-insider pointed out the need to maintain "a multifaceted network for enhancing stimulation." He put this more prosaically: "If I did not have the diverse networks I have outside my company, I would go crazy."

True Change Doesn't Happen by Itself

As I have emphasized throughout this book, outsider-insiders reside at all levels of an organization, including executive ranks, and many are career two-hatters. The skill set associated with finding opportunities to pull in change does not get lost as one progresses up the hierarchy; with support, it only gets stronger. Particular outsider ideas may become obsolete, but the ability to wear two hats is not time, position, or situation dependent. Indeed, executive outsider-insiders who have earlier in their careers used their two hats to solve working-level problems have a much deeper understanding of the complexity of true change. They appreciate the difficulties facing other outsider-insiders within their organizations, especially those learning to wear two hats (they went through the process themselves), and they, like the rest of their fellow outsider-insiders, work to keep their own two hats in balance. This is not simple, as I noted at the outset. An organization's capability for true change comprises many elements, some being essentially individual, others being more fully the responsibilities of the organization itself.

True change is based on three essential fundamentals: people (outsider-insiders) who are nurtured and aided (support infrastructure) in their search for gaps between current assumptions and the root cause of the challenges facing an organization (pull change). It is dynamic; it draws on individual and organizational commitment to real change and evolves as macro challenges arise and micro challenges persist. It must evolve as the organization grows and matures. There is no silver bullet for true change, much less a hoped-for pushcart to be wheeled in at times of crisis.

Even outsider-insiders within our two best practice cases often question whether their organizations are truly open to outsider perspectives. After all, many of them have become veteran outsider-insiders who are accustomed to questioning both their organization's and their personal assumptions. Although they can look around and count numerous success stories where they and their peers have introduced outsider perspectives to solve both macro and micro challenges, organizational assumptions are still deeply rooted and can pose what can appear to be monumental roadblocks, especially to developing outsider-insiders. Both BigFab and HiTech recognize that they are not perfect and must continually strive to improve their outsider-insider support infrastructures. They recognize that it is a continuous improvement process to help outsider-insiders maintain a balance between their two hats. And to their credit, and our edification, both companies have succeeded in building a critical mass of outsider-insiders at every level of the organizational hierarchy. These masses have become a powerful internal network dedicated to sponsoring and mentoring future generations of outsider-insiders to carry on the tradition of searching for opportunities to pull in change.

One could easily write off being an outsider-insider as a gene some people are just born with. But as we have seen throughout the book, it is much more constructed. It is a state of mind that needs continual refreshing and support for exploring alternative approaches or perspectives. As a result, organizations and outsider-insiders must be proactive in nurturing and maintaining a healthy balance between the two hats, even as the organization evolves. And then both must work together to find new and exciting forums to use those two hats. A BigFab executive outsider-insider succinctly noted, with passion, "You have to be able to be an outsider to see what needs to change. If I put on an insider hat, the ride is over. Being able to see what needs to change and get others to see it is my ticket to get to another show."

Appendix: Research Methodology

True Change emerged from analyzing the results of three inter-related research projects: (1) a five-year study exploring the transfer and utilization of new manufacturing concepts in twelve major corporations, (2) a three-year multidisciplinary study of the development and maintenance of high-performance globally dispersed teams, and (3) a two-year investigation into the ability of full-time employees to learn new concepts through distance education while being totally emerged within their organizations.

These projects were conducted under the auspices of the Leaders for Manufacturing (LFM) and System Design and Management (SDM) Partnership, a tripartite partnership between MIT's School of Engineering, Sloan School of Management, and numerous international manufacturing and engineering enterprises. The cornerstone of the partnership is two graduate programs. The LFM program's mission is to train future leaders of manufacturing enterprises in the principles of world-class operations, while the SDM program aims to educate future technical leaders in architecting, engineering, and designing complex products and systems.[1]

LFM Utilization Research Project

In 1994, I become the academic lead for the partnership's research group on Organization Culture, Learning and Change. The group was charged by the LFM governing board with investigating the impact of organizational culture on knowledge transfer. Given that the partnership was composed of a diverse set of corporations, we decided to study the program itself. Between 1995 and 1998, over 138 managers/executives and 144 alumni were interviewed to better understand the influence of organizational culture on LFM knowledge utilization in twelve large partner companies: three global automotive companies, one aerospace corporation, four electronics or high-technology firms, one material processing fabricator, two image processing manufacturers, and one highly diversified engineering and manufacturing enterprise.[2]

The interviews typically lasted one hour and covered the following topics:

- Stakeholder expectations versus reality
- Corporate LFM strategy (initial and changes over time)
- Perception of LFM students and alumni
- Experience with LFM students and alumni
- Diffusion of thesis learnings
- Recruiting goals and strategies
- Career planning/mentors
- Matching of job opportunities to skills and expectations
- Organizational culture (plant, division, corporate): receptivity to change, receptivity of new ideas, and processes for learning and diffusion of learning

Twelve extensive case studies were prepared and reviewed by each company. A comparative case analysis distilled common themes across the companies and identified two organizations, BigFab and HiTech (Company B and E, respectively, in Table A.1), to be best practice cases. Employment history then triangulated these findings. The two companies had created the largest critical mass of alumni in terms of both employees sponsored to return to school for development activities and new employees. Both companies also had outstanding retention rates, especially given the mobility and

Table A.1. Leaders for Manufacturing Retention by Partner Organization, October 2001

Company	Development of Critical Mass				Retention			
	New Employees	Sponsored	Postgraduate	Total	New Employees	Sponsored	Postgraduate	Total
B	18	21	1	40	72%	90%	100%	83%
E	31	22	6	59	81	77	67	78
G	11	9	2	22	64	100	50	77
I	17	2	2	21	53	100	100	62
L	4	23	1	28	100	52	100	61
J	8	3	0	11	50	67	0	55
K	20	1	1	22	45	0	100	45
H	7	8	1	16	29	50	100	44
A	15	6	2	23	47	17	100	43
F	12	3	0	15	33	67	0	40
C	1	4	0	5	0	50	0	40
D	8	6	1	15	25	0	0	13
Total partners	210	115	30	355	60	64	70	62

Note: To highlight differences across the twelve companies while still protecting anonymity, the companies were identified as Company A through L.

demand for individuals with similar credentials during the 1990s. In addition, a number of alumni had risen into executive-level positions (six at BigFab, three at HiTech), an indication that they had reached a level of influence within their organizations. Follow-up interviews with eleven senior alumni (those who had been back in the workforce for seven to twelve years postgraduation, including many of those in executive positions) were conducted during the fall of 2003 to ascertain the degree to which they were able to maintain their outsider perspectives over time.

The notion of outsider-insiders emerged from the case studies but was grounded in earlier references used to describe the educational experience. From the beginning of the partnership, graduates were marketed as being bilingual, meaning that they were able to manage both the engineering and business sides of the business. This naturally led to their being referred to as wearing two hats: engineering and management. Furthermore, in preparation for their internship, students were asked to consider whether they wanted to be a "Convert" and conform to the internship company's culture or remain a "Martian" and just observe it as a visitor during their six months within a company.[3] The concept of outsider-insiders, as used in this book, was an extension of these earlier references but did not emerge until after the comparative case study analysis. Hence, no attempt was made to distinguish outsider-insiders from insiders during the interview process. In retrospect, both groups, managers and alumni, were composed of a mix of outsider-insiders and insiders.

Multidisciplinary Research on Globally Dispersed Teams

From 1998 to 2001, I was the academic lead for a multidisciplinary research project investigating the development and maintenance of high-performance globally dispersed teams (GDTs). The research was sponsored by Visteon and Intel, two industrial partners within the LFM/SDM Partnership, and explored a range of topics, including:

- How globally dispersed teams come together and achieve high performance
- Leadership role in effective teams where members are physically dispersed
- How to build relationships in teams that are not colocated
- Preparatory steps and management actions that enhance the success of globally dispersed teams
- The roles of technology, organizational processes, and physical and digital space on facilitating collaboration
- Criteria defining effective and efficient collaboration practices for global teams

This research included literature reviews, surveys, and in-depth case studies. Beyond that, the research team participated in interactive forums that linked managers and researchers across multiple companies and universities around the world.[4] Becoming ourselves a virtual learning team, we met using multiple communication vehicles (including face-to-face, video- and audioconferencing, and groupware) to exchange ideas about best practices, share research findings, and identify issues for future research. We used ourselves as a laboratory to test the validity of our research findings.

This project was composed of researchers who were born and raised or lived for a significant amount of time in seventeen countries in North and South America, Europe, Africa, Asia, and Australia. Their findings contributed to eight doctoral dissertations and thirty-two master's theses in management or engineering. Many of the researchers, who were students in MIT's Sloan Fellows and Management of Technology executive education programs, had also either extensive experience as members or leaders of GDTs or held expatriate assignments. Their experiences led us to realize that virtual collaboration provided another avenue to learn to wear two hats.

A key theme that emerged from the global team research was the tension between local and global strategies and priorities, thereby requiring GDT members to learn to live in two worlds simultaneously.[5] Numerous case studies highlighted the influence of push versus pull strategies on the acceptance of global best practices at the local level as well.

SDM Distance Learning and Utilization Research Project

In 1997, MIT created the System Design and Management (SDM) program, its first distance-learning degree program, where students earn a joint degree in engineering and management in the field of system design and product development. Like LFM, it is a partnership between MIT and several major corporations that sponsor students for both full-time study on campus and off-campus (videoconference and Web-based) distance learning. In 2000, NASA and Ford provided research funding to apply what we had learned in the prior two studies to the SDM program to develop advanced distance education capabilities and enhance the utilization of SDM competencies (systems engineering) within the SDM sponsor organizations. This also gave us a platform to explore how employees learned to question their assumptions while holding full-time jobs, typically ones that were of a very technical nature.

The research included longitudinal surveys of students at six-month intervals over a two-year period and in-depth case studies on three partner organizations (similar in nature to the LFM utilization case studies). The survey used in the GDT research was modified to explore distance education aspects of the program. It validated the importance of a support infrastructure to help insiders learn to wear two hats and the application of new concepts at the workplace For example, Table A.2 illustrates that there is indeed a significant correlation between the perceived existence and use of a support infrastructure and the expected utilization of new skills acquired in the SDM program. Furthermore, Table A.3 shows that respondents indicated that learning new concepts and questioning assumptions at a distance was easier when students felt part of a strong student cohort and had organizational support for applying their new competencies within their organizations.

■ ■ ■

The findings from all three studies are now being used by the LFM/SDM partnership to enhance the educational experience and help partner organizations better utilize alumni upon return or entry into their firms. The lessons, articulated in *True Change*, have also been incorporated into the program's curriculum to help students understand their role in learning to be a proactive outsider-insider in finding and leveraging opportunities to pull in change.

Table A.2. Survey Responses at End of Two-Year SDM Distance Education Program

The skills I acquire in the SDM program will be effectively utilized by my organization.	Pearson Correlation	Significance (two-tailed)	N
My organization provides excellent support (e.g., training staff, help desks) for using communication technologies.	0.775	0.000	36
My local supervisor understands why my organization is part of the SDM program.	0.674	0.000	39
Organization leadership is actively involved in my progress through the SDM program.	0.582	0.000	40
My local supervisor understands the objectives of the SDM program.	0.531	0.000	40
Being in the SDM program has a negative impact on my performance evaluation on my job.	-0.531	0.000	39
My organization provides sufficient links or networks back to the organization for on-campus students.	0.499	0.001	38
I report to the top management at my site about the SDM program on a regular basis.	0.486	0.001	40
My local supervisor is actively involved in my progress throughout the SDM program.	0.471	0.002	40
My organization does not understand how to support employees when they are in the SDM program.	-0.665	0.003	18
My organization has made it clear what is required for future career development and lifelong learning post-SDM.	0.460	0.003	40
I would consider leaving my organization for better opportunities upon completion of the program.	-0.470	0.003	38
My coworkers understand the objectives of the SDM program.	0.642	0.004	18
My supervisor provides opportunities to incorporate new ideas that are taught in SDM.	0.639	0.004	18

The skills I acquire in the SDM program will be effectively utilized by my organization.	Pearson Correlation	Significance (two-tailed)	N
I feel comfortable talking to my local supervisor about the SDM program.	0.440	0.005	39
My supervisor does not understand how to support its employees when they are in the SDM program.	-0.434	0.006	39
I receive official recognition from my organization for being in the SDM program.	0.429	0.006	40
Organization leadership does not understand the major concerns facing employees in the SDM program.	-0.428	0.007	39
Being in the SDM program has a positive impact on my performance evaluation on my job.	0.415	0.009	39
During my performance reviews, my supervisor takes into account the application of SDM concepts and tools as part of my evaluation.	0.565	0.018	17
Organizational leadership understands the objectives of the SDM program.	0.542	0.020	18
I have a mentor who coaches me on how to best link my SDM experience to the organization.	0.366	0.020	40
Local needs take priority over SDM requirements.	-0.358	0.025	39
My organization is fully committed to supporting me through the completion of my SDM course work.	0.327	0.042	39
My coworkers encourage efforts to incorporate new ideas that are taught in SDM.	0.476	0.046	18

Table A.3. SDM Survey Responses, June 2002

Exploration of new ideas off campus (alpha = .8304)

I am better able to understand the relevance of what I have learned to current or future jobs when I'm off campus than when I'm on campus.
I am better able to question my assumptions (mental models) while off campus than on campus.
I can more easily learn new concepts (ways of doing/thinking) off campus than on campus.

	Pearson Correlation	Significance (two-tailed)	N
Virtual presence and cohort			
As a remote student, I feel part of the class environment.	0.585	0.036	13
The business trip promotes the development of relationships among students.	0.593	0.033	13
The business trip has a positive impact on the classroom interaction between remote and on-campus students.	0.617	0.025	13
The business trip has a positive impact on the classroom interaction between faculty and remote students.	0.685	0.010	13
I have used the MIT resources available to me as a SDM student (databases, online library, e-journals, etc.).	0.631	0.021	13
Organizational support			
I depend on the local site budget to support my SDM activities.	−0.604	0.038	12
My organization has made it clear what is required for future career development and lifelong learning post-SDM.	0.638	0.025	12
The skills I acquire in the SDM program will be effectively utilized by my organization.	0.739	0.009	11
I have applied my SDM learning directly to my job.	0.755	0.003	13
Organization leadership does not understand the major concerns facing employees in the SDM program.	−0.718	0.009	12

Notes

Chapter One

1. Christensen, C. *The Innovator's Dilemma: The Revolutionary Book That Will Change the Way You Do Business.* New York: HarperBusiness, 1997.
2. The term "outsiders on the inside" has been used in a number of contexts. For example, it was used during the late 1970s and early 1980s to refer to women within organizations. See Forisha, B., and Goldman, F. *Outsiders on the Inside: Women and Organizations.* Upper Saddle River, N.J.: Prentice Hall, 1980. It is also used in politics to refer to newcomers to the political scene.
3. See the appendix for additional background on the research projects.
4. I am indebted to one of the blind referees for this book who, on reading the draft manuscript, observed that the book was really about building an organizational change capability through the development and use of outsider-insiders.
5. There is a rich history of outstanding change management research, for example, Lewin, K. "Group Decision and Social Change." In T. Newcomb and E. Hartley (eds.), *Readings in Social Psychology.* New York: Holt, 1947; Beckhard, R., and Harris, R. *Organizational Transitions: Managing Complex Change.* Reading, Mass.: Addison-Wesley, 1987; Schein, E. *Organizational Culture and Leadership.* San Francisco: Jossey-Bass, 1992. The work of Noel Tichy also explores the concept of bridging current and

innovative practice; most recently, Tichy, N. *The Cycle of Leadership: How Great Leaders Teach Their Companies to Win.* New York: HarperBusiness, 2002. Unfortunately, much of the more popular literature on change management is heavily weighted toward quick-fix formulas or anecdotal success stories.

6. Adapted from Klein, J. "The Council Bluffs Plant (A)." Harvard Business School Case Study No. 9–688–111, 1988.

7. Weick, K. "Small Wins." *American Psychologist,* 1984, *39*(1), 40–49.

8. The concept here is similar to idea practitioners Davenport, T., and Prusak, L. *What's the Big Idea? Creating and Capitalizing on the Best Management Thinking.* Boston: Harvard Business School Press, 2003. But idea practitioners are staff people who need outsider-insiders to find opportunities to pull in the ideas they find.

9. Campbell, J., *The Hero with a Thousand Faces.* Princeton, N.J.: Princeton University Press. 1949; Bennis, W., and Thomas, R. *Geeks and Geezers: How Era, Values, and Defining Moments Shape Leaders.* Boston: Harvard Business School Press, 2002.

10. See the appendix for metrics for success, such as number of outsider-insiders, their level of influence with each company, and retention.

Chapter Two

1. Schein, E. *Organizational Culture and Leadership.* San Francisco: Jossey-Bass, 1992.

2. Vaughan, D. *The Challenger Launch Decision: Risky Technology, Culture, and Deviance at NASA.* Chicago: University of Chicago Press, 1996.

3. Heifetz, R. *Leadership Without Easy Answers.* Cambridge, Mass.: Harvard University Press, 1994.

4. Beckhard, R., and Harris, R. *Organizational Transitions: Managing Complex Change.* Reading, Mass.: Addison-Wesley, 1987.

Chapter Three

1. There is a rich strategic management literature that addresses competitive responses to environmental changes that is outside the scope of this book. See, for example, Porter, M. *Competitive Advantage: Creating and Sustaining Superior Performance.* New York: Free Press, 1985.

2. For further background on the Sedalia Engine Plant, see Harvard Business School case studies, "Sedalia Engine Plant (A)," No. 9–481–148, 1981, and "Sedalia Revisited," No. 9–687–004, 1986; Klein, J. "The Human Costs of Manufacturing Reform." *Harvard Business Review,* Mar.–Apr. 1989, pp. 60–66; Klein, J. "A Reexamination of Autonomy in Light of New Manufacturing Practices." *Human Relations,* 1991, *44*(1), 21–38.

3. Creating alignment around a clear vision and need for change is the cornerstone of most change management texts. Full example, see Kantor, R., Stein, B., and Jick, T. *The Challenge of Organizational Change: How Companies Experience It and Leaders Guide It.* New York: Free Press, 1992; Kotter, J. *Leading Change.* Boston: Harvard Business School Press, 1996; and Tichy, N., and Devanna, M. *The Transformational Leader.* New York: Wiley, 1986; or Beer, M., Eisenstat, R., and Spector, B. *The Critical Path to Corporate Renewal.* Boston: Harvard Business School Press, 1990. The key distinction here is the need to align in the processes for change in addition to the need for change.

4. Gerstner, L. *Who Says Elephants Can't Dance?* New York: HarperBusiness, 2002.

Chapter Four

1. This is a classic chicken-and-egg scenario. Most change management scholars emphasize the need for cultural transformations to reinforce change efforts (for example, Goodman, P.,

and Associates. *Change in Organizations*. San Francisco: Jossey-Bass, 1982; Beer, M., Eisenstat, R., and Spector, B. *The Critical Path to Corporate Renewal*. Boston: Harvard Business School Press, 1990) and recognize the need to work within the existing culture to effect change, but little research has been done on the idea of leveraging the existing culture to change it.

2. A classic article on how organizations evolve is Greiner, L. "Evolution and Revolution as Organizations Grow." *Harvard Business Review*, July–Aug. 1972, pp. 37–46.

3. Meyerson, D. *Tempered Radicals: How People Use Difference to Inspire Change at Work*. Boston: Harvard Business School Press, 2001.

4. See the appendix for metrics for success in building critical mass of outsider-insiders.

Chapter Five

1. See, for example, Caligiuri, P., and Lazarova, M. "Strategic Repatriation Policies to Enhance Global Leadership Development." In M. Mendenhall, T. Kuehlmann, and G. Stahl (eds.), *Developing Global Business Leaders: Policies, Processes, and Innovations*. Westport, Conn.: Quorum Books, 2001.

2. Klein, J., and Barrett, B. "One Foot in a Global Team, One Foot at the Local Site: Making Sense Out of Living in Two Worlds Simultaneously." In M. Beyerlein and D. Johnson (eds.), *Advances in Interdisciplinary Studies of Work Teams*, Vol. 8: *Virtual Teams*. Stamford, Conn.: JAI-Elsevier, 2001; Black, J., and Gregersen, H. "Serving Two Masters: The Dual Allegiance of Expatriate Employees." *Sloan Management Review*, 1992, 33(4), 61–71.

3. Meyerson, D., Weick, K., and Kramer, R. "Swift Trust and Temporary Groups." In R. Kramer and T. Tyler (eds.), *Trust in Organizations: Frontiers of Theory and Research*. Thousand Oaks, Calif.: Sage, 1996.

4. Klein and Barrett, 2001.

5. This example is based on a conversation with Julie Rennecker.
6. Klein, J., and Kleinhanns, A. "Closing the Time Gap in Virtual Teams." In C. Gibson and S. Cohen (eds.), *Virtual Teams at Work: Creating Conditions for Virtual Team Effectiveness.* San Francisco: Jossey-Bass, 2003.
7. Black, J., Gregersen, H., and Mendenhall, M. *Global Assignments.* San Francisco: Jossey-Bass, 1992.
8. See the appendix for further information on research.
9. Baughn, C. "Personal and Organizational Factors Associated with Effective Repatriation." In J. Selma (ed.), *Expatriate Management: New Ideas for International Business.* Westport, Conn.: Quorum Books, 1995.

Chapter Six

1. This is similar to shift credibility. Meyerson, D., Weick, K., and Kramer, R. "Swift Trust and Temporary Groups." In R. Kramer and T. Tyler (eds.), *Trust in Organizations: Frontiers of Theory and Research.* Thousand Oaks, Calif.: Sage, 1996.

Chapter Seven

1. See for example, Davenport, T., and Prusak, L. *Working Knowledge: How Organizations Manage What They Know.* Boston: Harvard Business School Press, 2000; Gladwell, M. *The Tipping Point: How Little Things Can Make a Big Difference.* New York: Little, Brown, 2000.
2. See, for example, Kram, K. *Mentoring at Work: Developmental Relationships in Organizational Life.* Lanham, Md.: University Press of America, 1988; McCall, M. *High Flyers: Developing the Next Generation of Leaders.* Boston: Harvard Business School Press, 1988.
3. Dan's story is based on personal interviews and published descriptions of his managerial style, including Johansen, T., and Litzen, U. "Globally Dispersed Teams in a Strategic Context."

Unpublished Sloan Fellows thesis, Massachusetts Institute of Technology, 2001.

4. This is an example of swift trust. For further details, see Meyerson, D., Weick, K., and Kramer, R. "Swift Trust and Temporary Groups." In R. Kramer and T. Tyler (eds.), *Trust in Organizations: Frontiers of Theory and Research*. Thousand Oaks, Calif.: Sage, 1996.

Chapter Eight

1. This chapter is based in part on eleven interviews with veteran outsider-insiders. See the appendix for more details on the research methodology.

2. This is similar to creating a holding environment to channel stresses produced while introducing new ideas in less-than-friendly environments. For example, see Heifetz, R. *Leadership Without Easy Answers*. Cambridge, Mass.: Harvard University Press, 1994.

Appendix

1. For additional background, go to http://lfmsdm.mit.edu.

2. Many of the alumni were also managers, but all alumni were grouped together to distinguish them from managers and supervisors who were not graduates of the program.

3. Davis, F. "The Martian and the Convert." *Urban Life and Culture*, 1973, 2(3), 335–338, 342–343.

4. The forums included researchers from MIT and the Norwegian University of Science and Technology and managers from Visteon, Intel, and Norsk Hydro.

5. Klein, J., and Barrett, B. "One Foot in a Global Team, One Foot at the Local Site: Making Sense Out of Living in Two Worlds Simultaneously." In M. Beyerlein and D. Johnson (eds.), *Advances in Interdisciplinary Studies of Work Teams*, Vol. 8: *Virtual Teams*. Stamford, Conn.: JAI-Elsevier, 2001.

Index

The Author

Janice A. Klein is a senior lecturer at MIT's Sloan School of Management, where she teaches courses in operations management and leadership. Her earlier research focused on aligning operations and human resource strategies in the areas of job design, team leadership, employee empowerment, and organizational change. Her publications include "Why Supervisors Resist Employee Involvement" (*Harvard Business Review*, Aug.–Sept. 1984), "The Human Costs of Manufacturing Reform" (*Harvard Business Review*, Mar.–Apr., 1989), "A Reexamination of Autonomy in Light of New Manufacturing Practices" (*Human Relations*, 1991), "Maintaining Expertise in Multi-Skilled Teams (in M. Beyerlein and D. Johnson, eds., *Theories of Self-Managed Work Teams*, 1994), and "Job Design" (in R. C. Dorf, ed., *The Handbook of Technology Management*, 1998).

From 1983 to 1991, Klein was a member of the Production and Operations Management Faculty at the Harvard Business School. Her textbook, *Revitalizing Manufacturing: Text and Cases* (1990), is a compilation of the material she developed in the Management of Operations, a course that focused on the implementation of new manufacturing systems and technologies.

From 1972 to 1981, Klein worked for General Electric, holding various manufacturing and human resource management positions. In addition, she coordinated several organizational change efforts aimed at increasing employee involvement.

Klein received her B.S. in industrial engineering from Iowa State University, M.B.A. from Boston University, and Ph.D. in industrial relations from MIT's Sloan School of Management.

Printed in the United States
By Bookmasters